*beyond*Gorp

Favorite Foods from Outdoor Experts

beyond **Gorp**

Yvonne Prater and
Ruth Dyar Mendenhall
with Kerry I. Smith

THE MOUNTAINEERS BOOKS

THE MOUNTAINEERS BOOKS
is the nonprofit publishing arm of The Mountaineers Club,
an organization founded in 1906 and dedicated to the exploration,
preservation, and enjoyment of outdoor and wilderness areas.

1001 SW Klickitat Way, Suite 201, Seattle, WA 98134

© 2005 by Yvonne Prater and Ruth Dyar Mendenhall

Published simultaneously in Great Britain by Cordee, 3a DeMontfort Street, Leicester, England, LE1 7HD

Manufactured in the United States of America

Project Editor: Laura Drury
Editor: Uma Kukathas
Cover, Book Design, and Layout: Mayumi Thompson
Illustrator: Judy Shimono

Cover photograph: © Getty Images

Library of Congress Cataloging-in-Publication Data
    Prater, Yvonne, 1932-
Favorite foods from outdoor experts / Yvonne Prater and Ruth Dyar
Mendenhall, with Kerry I. Smith.— 1st ed.
    p. cm.
  Includes index.
  ISBN 0-89886-890-4
  1. Outdoor cookery. I. Mendenhall, Ruth. II. Smith , Kerry I. III. Title.
TX823.P6897 2005
641.5'78—dc22
                                        2004021304

Contents

• • • • • • • • •

preface

*O*utdoor activities such as hiking, climbing, skiing, snowshoeing, and kayaking always result in a combination of exhilaration, fatigue, and *hunger*. Drawing upon the success of the book *Gorp, Glop and Glue Stew,* which Ruth and I published in 1982, this book is devised to keep you well fed when you are outdoors doing the things you love.

> ✗ This book is a collection of classic recipes and stories, noted with the icon on the left, from Gorp, as well as new contributions—many by well-known outdoors folk from several continents. Their culinary talents, insights, wisdom, and wit are sure to "hit the spot."

Several of the recipes are well-loved favorites that have been handed down from one generation to the next. Others are favorites that have been adapted to make them easier to prepare on the trail, in locations around the world. Some of them have become standards made and shared at family gatherings, backyard potlucks, and county fairs.

The recipes in this book include snacks to keep your energy from waning, dishes that are prepared at home and then cooked in camp, wild food feasts, and good food with little work. Adaptations of ethnic concoctions might bring back fond memories of a favorite climb in a faraway land. You will also find lots of hints on how to add a little variety to your menu on the trail.

We hope that this book will inspire imaginative cooks who recognize a good recipe when they read one, whether or not they are outdoor adventurers. Who knows, you may become the designated chef on your next outing.

One more thing: be sure to stash the book in your pack…the real-life stories shared by these well-known outdoor adventurers may lead to some yarn-spinning of your own.

From kitchen to trail, have a splendid adventure!

acknowledgments

A project of this complexity takes a while to complete. I would like to express my deep gratitude to the following people for their interest, enthusiasm, and expertise in helping with this book. Louise Marshall, founder of *Signposts* magazine, for her brilliant suggestion that Ruth and I include in our cookery book not only recipes, but anecdotes and biographies of well-known outdoors people as well.

My coauthor, the late Ruth Dyar Mendenhall, who passed away in 1989, only seven years after *Gorp, Glop & Glue Stew's* publication. I'll bet she is smiling now, happy to see the book not only endure twelve printings but become the basis for a new book.

Each of the book's contributors, for believing in the project and for the time spent combing through personal recipes and cooking ideas, sharing stories, and—even more difficult—writing a biography of themselves.

Dorcas Miller, an outdoor cookbook guru herself, who captured the essence of this book in the introduction. Thanks are extended too for her helpful tips.

The staff at The Mountaineers Books: Helen Cherullo, publisher, Deb Easter, editor, and Kathleen Cubley, managing editor, for encouraging me to update *Gorp*; Uma Kukathas, copyeditor, Laura Drury, editor; Cheryl Landes, indexer; Mayumi Thompson, book designer; the marketing team; Christine Grabowski and Anne Moreau, interns, the super-sleuths who diligently tracked down many of the original contributors to obtain updated biographies and researched trail food lore; and those who sacrificed off-duty hours to test the recipes in their own kitchens and outdoors—Helen Cherullo, Deb Easter, Kathleen Cubley, Alison Koop, Hally Swift, Tim Warne, and Elaine Bongiorno.

Additional recipe testers, Kymmberly Myrick, Hannah Myrick, Toni MacAdam, Merrill Hayden, and Helga Byhre; thanks to Merrill and Helga for their recipes as well, found on pages 126 and 132, respectively.

Finally to Kerry Smith, the writer who shared the vision of a renewed life for *Gorp*, for her tenacity in soliciting new contributions, and for making the difficult decisions about which recipes would make the "final cut."

Yvonne Prater

Introduction

By Dorcas Miller

*B*efore setting out on a canoe trip in the North Maine Woods, my friend Elaine and I agreed that I would pack breakfasts, she would pack lunches, and we would split the dinners. It was a great plan. But on day one when she pulled out a big bag of carrot and celery sticks, a container of hummus, and a little box of crackers, I knew I was in trouble.

I travel on my stomach.

With thirty-one calories per whole carrot; six per celery stalk; twen̶t̶y̶ per tablespoon of hummus; and fifteen (more or less, depend̶ brand) per cracker, there was not nearly enough fuel to keep me ̶ dinner, on that day or the days following. It was the only time t̶ been consistently hungry on trail, and I'm looking at thirty-fou̶ backcountry eating. With carrot sticks in mind, I've rarely relinqui̶s̶ trol over how much and what type of food goes into the commun̶a̶

An adequate amount of tasty food, a warm sleeping bag, and̶ fortable sleeping pad go a long way toward attaining backcoun̶ vana. (So does good weather, but that's outside my realm.) Fo̶ make or break an outing—it can provide a potent antidote to m̶ toes, blisters, sore muscles, and a heavy pack.

What's key to planning and packing trail food? The most important thing to understand, says foodie Jean Spangenberg—and as a development specialist at Adventure Foods she feeds thousands of hikers each year—is to treat your body as your most important piece of equipment. Typically, outdoor enthusiasts spend hours deliberating over which tent to purchase, but then buy food the night before the trip, or pour money into lightweight, high-tech gear only to scrimp on meals. If you flip the order of priorities and make food a top concern, your body will rejoice.

Some years back I did a "make over" for a backpacking couple, assessing what they took on an (unhappy) five-day trip and making suggestions for their next outing. I told them:

- **Take food you like.** Don't assume that everything tastes better outdoors. If you don't like oatmeal at home, you won't like it on trail.
- **This is your vacation.** Treat yourself. Spend a little extra to get good quality food, and pack items that you especially enjoy—roasted

cashews, dried cherries, lush chocolate, full-flavored coffee.

- **Plan ahead.** Three meals a day don't appear by magic. Once you've left the launch site, you can't easily buy items you have forgotten. Figure out amounts per person.
- **What you have on your shelf may not be what you want on your trip.** Don't take something simply because it's handy.
- **Consider calories.** How many you need will depend on the activity, the weather, your size, and your metabolism. You won't burn as many on a laid-back summer day as you will on an uphill grind in the winter.
- **Plan menus for variety.** For lunch and snacks, include items with different tastes and textures, such as crunchy/salty (pretzels, fish crackers, salted nuts), crunchy/sweet (animal crackers, cookies), chewy/salty (jerky), chewy/sweet (dried fruit), rich/creamy (nut butters), and rich/chewy (cheese).
- **Keep variety in mind for other meals as well.** Garnish a one-pot stew with a handful of toasted nuts (crunchy) or a sprig of fresh cilantro (flavorful). Include tortillas (chewy and delicious warmed with a little butter). Use herbs and spices (packets of ginger/lemon grass or pad Thai seasoning will make your taste buds zing.)
- **Take advantage of the wide array of light, quick-prep food that is available these days.** Then, doctor the mundane. Serve pasta with rehydrated tomatoes and mushrooms, fresh pesto (if kept cool, pesto can be unrefrigerated up to 24 hours), and Parmesan cheese. Or, serve wheat pilaf with freeze-dried corn, bacon, onion, and cheddar.
- **Have fun. Is someone going to celebrate a birthday on the trip?** Make a cake or pack treats from the bakery.
- **Consider your habits when on the trail.** Do you like leisurely breakfasts? Pancakes are a good slow-start meal. Prefer a quick cold breakfast? Pack homemade granola or breakfast bars with lots of fruit, nuts, and calories.
- **Consider the unexpected.** Even if you anticipate an unhurried trip, carry at least one quick-cooking dinner to allow for the unforeseen.
- **Include directions with every breakfast and dinner.** Just because you planned the food doesn't mean you have to prepare it.
- **Keep track of what works and what doesn't.** What was the favorite meal of the trip? The least favorite? Was the quantity right? Did that chili need more pep? Make notes on your menu and recipes (yes, keep a copy of your menu and recipes). Three months later, when you're planning the next trip, you'll appreciate the detail.

Learning from the success of others is as important as learning from their mistakes. This book, packed with favorite recipes from dozens of trail veterans, provides a jump-start to planning. A cruise through the pages turns up foods that I'd love to find in my pack.

Mountain McMuffins—the name foretells the ingredients (ham, eggs, hollandaise sauce, muffins, and cheese)—promise stamina well beyond plain oatmeal.

Canyon Crostinis pair rounds of toasted bread with an appetizing dip. Alaska Smoked Salmon Pasta can hardly go wrong, providing pasta for glycogen and salmon, capers, garlic, and other ingredients to woo taste buds.

A fruity Snow Cake (not to be confused with fruitcake) features dates, raisins, cranberries and apricots, all flavored with ginger and cardamom. Trail Tiramisu blends unexciting instant chocolate pudding with potent Kahlua and espresso, and layers the mix with dainty ladyfingers and shaved chocolate.

One of my goals on the trail is to eat as well as I do at home. With recipes like these, I might wind up eating better in the backcountry.

How Much to Pack?

If you don't know how much you eat in the backcountry, the next time you have a one-pot meal, measure the amount you ladle onto your plate and think about how much more you'd want if you'd been on the trail all day. If you don't know how much your partner eats, ask. For a not-so-demanding trip, I generally plan three cups per male and two cups per female for dinner.

Those Wiley Calories

There are a couple of ways to figure out whether you're packing enough BTUs. The first is to count calories, a project made easier by the abundance of calorie booklets in the supermarket and nutritional labels on packaged products. The second is to use the National Outdoor Leadership School's rule of thumb concerning weight. (Packing by weight assumes that you have a mix of dehydrated, freeze-dried, and whole food items.)

The third avenue is to make sure that you provide carbs, protein, and fats at each meal or snack, or balanced over a day. Carbohydrates are good for producing glycogen and quick energy. Protein is used in re-building muscles. Fats provide longer-term energy, a sense of satisfaction, and more than twice the number of calories per weight than either carbs or protein.

- For a day of normal hiking and paddling—an average day outdoors—you may need about 2500 to 3000 calories, or about 1½ to 2 pounds of food per person.

- For a day of strenuous activity, you may need 3000 to 3700 calories, or about 2 to 2¼ pounds per person.
- For a full day of all-out mountaineering, you may need 3700 to 4500 calories, or 2¼ to 2½ pounds per person.

Camp Kitchens: Minimizing Impact

Follow Leave No Trace (LNT) principles when setting up your camp kitchen and cleaning up after meals. Camp in well used sites whenever possible.

- Choose an area with a durable surface (such as rock or hardened ground) that can withstand foot traffic.
- Set up shop 200 feet from rivers or lakes.
- Use a camp stove instead of a fire.
- Pick up food scraps that land on the ground.
- Develop a taste for post-entree broth: pour hot water into your bowl, swish it around and savor. The broth helps you rehydrate and clears your bowl.
- If you must use soap, use a biodegradable product. Wash on another durable surface, about 200 feet from the kitchen.
- Strain wash water with a bit of screening and pack out the remnants.
- Scatter water on durable ground.
- When in bear country, store food, kitchen items, garbage, and anything with a fragrance (toothpaste, hand lotion, and so on) in a bear box, or hang it from a rope or line.

Fresh Food

You don't have to carry the entire produce bin. Just a few fresh items a day can give your meals a lift.

- Pack fragile foods in your bowl or cookset.
- Choose fruits and vegetables loaded with flavor, texture, and fragrance, such as a ripe avocado, a crisp Braeburn apple, or a clove of pungent garlic.
- Target produce that can withstand the rigors of trail life. Cabbage, citrus fruits, onions, garlic, and carrots last longest and are practically impervious to rough treatment. Apples will also last well if properly cushioned. Avocados, mushrooms, bell peppers, snap peas, and summer squash can last three to five days. Peaches, plums, bananas, green beans, and broccoli should be eaten on the first or second day.
- Cut produce when you are ready to use it. If you prep produce at home, it will lose flavor and nutrients—and spoil—faster.
- Fruits and vegetables need to breathe; pack them in a paper, cloth, or perforated plastic bag.

Measuring

Exact measurements are important in baked goods, though not critical or necessary in many other types of recipes. All measurements in this book are standard American cookbook measurements, except for those found in the chapter "Ethnic Adaptations," beginning on page 185. Measurements for ethnic foods are given in the metric system, if that is the system used in the country of origin for a particular recipe.

1 cup = 8 fluid ounces
1 quart = 32 fluid ounces (4 standard measuring cups)
1 liter = 1.057 quarts, liquid measure
1 gram = .035 ounces; 100 grams = 3.5 ounces
1 kilogram = 2.2 pounds
1 teaspoon means a level teaspoonful
1 tablespoon, also level = 3 teaspoons
4 tablespoons = ¼ cup or 2 ounces

In some recipes, both the weight (in ounces or pounds) and the fluid measurement are given, for convenience.

Oven temperatures are given in degrees Fahrenheit (°F). Note: Drinking cups used in camp are nearly always larger than standard 8-ounce measuring cups, and camp spoons are usually larger than those found in the home kitchen.

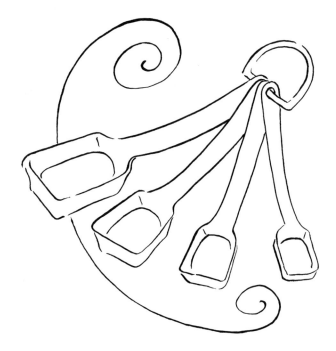

Cooking at Elevation

Elevation influences food preparation in various ways. The most noticeable effect is the extra time required to prepare boiled foods. At sea level, water boils at 212°F; at 5000 feet elevation, at 203°F; at 10,000 feet, at 194°F. In practical terms, the cooking time for many boiled foods doubles with every 5000 feet of elevation gain—and some foods will never get cooked at high altitudes because the decrease in atmospheric pressure lowers the boiling point, allowing the water to boil at too low a temperature for convenient cooking.

The cooking time for baked foods does not vary much with altitude, but as the barometric pressure drops with increasing elevations, leavening agents, such as baking powder, become more active. In camp baking, no correction is needed when you bake. Just enjoy the extra fluffiness of your baked foods. It is a beneficial offset to unpredictable conditions such as fluctuating temperatures.

See Chester Rice's tips for planning food for an outing and his cooking advice, page 82.

Daybreak: Breakfasts

*B*eing well fed at the beginning of the day adds to the pleasure ahead of you. There are plenty of options in this chapter to get even the grumpiest camper out of the sleeping bag and revved up to go.

Regardless of whether you like to have a breakfast extravaganza—complete with scrambled eggs and muffins, or pancakes with fruit—or prefer to keep it simple with a bowl of hearty couscous or granola, there are plenty of choices here. And if you need more to select from, take a look at the chapter "Energizing Snacks, Breads, and Lunches," beginning on page 47, for more ideas.

It's a new day, so rise and shine!

Kristin Hostetter

Cascade Morning Couscous

1 cup whole-wheat couscous
2 cups water
1 handful dried fruit (raisins, dried apples, dried coconut, or
    peaches)
Spices, to taste (cinnamon and/or nutmeg)
Brown sugar, to taste

Bring water to boil. Add the fruit and boil for a few minutes. Stir in the couscous and spices. Let stand, covered, for 5 minutes. Fluff with a fork, then sprinkle with sugar. Serves 1.

• • • • • • • • • •

Kristin Hostetter was *Backpacker* magazine's equipment editor for seven years. Aside from enjoying full-time momhood (two boys, Charlie and Joe), she currently writes a monthly column for *Backpacker* called "Ask Kristin," and a bimonthly column for the *Seattle Post-Intelligencer* called "Gearing Up." She is the author of *Don't Forget The Duct Tape: Tips and Tricks for Repairing Outdoor Gear* (The Mountaineers Books) and *Backpacker Adventure Journal* (The Mountaineers Books). Kristin lives in Milton, Massachusetts.

"When you've had enough of oatmeal, try this delicious breakfast. On dozens of gear testing trips for Backpacker *magazine, this breakfast—along with some strong, dark coffee—really revved my testing crews' engines."*

See Kristin's recipe for Rodeo Rice, page 92, and Off-Piste Pesto Pasta, page 119.

Ted Millan

Angry Moose Scrambled Eggs

10 cups water
2 cups dried potatoes
2 cups dried ham
2 cups grated cheddar cheese
4 heaping tablespoons dried mixed vegetables (sweet pepper, onion, broccoli, tomato)
8 tablespoons powdered eggs
Salt and pepper, to taste

Place all ingredients except the eggs in a frying pan or pot. Bring slowly to a boil. Cover and simmer for 10 to 15 minutes, stirring frequently. If the mix is too dry, add water as needed in small amounts. When the vegetables and ham are rehydrated, sprinkle eggs evenly over the mix. Stir until thoroughly blended. Remove from heat. Add salt and pepper. Serves 8 to 10.

For faster cooking, re-hydrate the potatoes and ham in a resealable plastic bag overnight if serving for breakfast, or while you make camp if serving for dinner.

. . . .

"Angry Moose Scrambled Eggs is an evolving recipe, once served on a fifty-mile outing in the Buckhorn Wilderness of Idaho. After an afternoon hike, I returned to camp and put the ingredients in water to rehydrate and simmer. I decided to take a quick dip in a nearby lake, so left the water on the stove and headed for the lake. I found the water refreshing, but then I noticed a moose gathering dinner about fifty yards away. Suddenly he arose out of the water and glared at me. Knowing that moose tend to have ill tempers, I left in a hurry. The moose didn't seem to mind, but I was spooked. When I got back to the stove, I went ahead with dinner, and added too much salt. The ham and salt combined made the meal very salty. The boys were hungry and didn't seem to mind, but they haven't let me forget the story."

See Ted's recipe for Makemwait Mushrooms, page 90, and Old Goats' One-Pot Ginger Cashew Chicken Fried Rice, page 102. "Ted Millan's Trail Food–Drying Basics" can be found on page 221. His biography appears on page 90.

Paul Charlton

Glacier Granola

10 cups oats
1 cup wheat germ*
1 cup shredded or flaked coconut
2 cups raw sunflower seeds
1 cup sesame seeds
3 cups nuts (your choice)
1½ cups brown sugar
1½ cups water
¾ cup oil
1 cup honey
½ teaspoon salt
2 teaspoons cinnamon
1 tablespoon vanilla

*According to one recipe tester, eliminating the wheat germ does not diminish the success or taste of the final product.

Combine the oats, wheat germ, coconut, sunflower seeds, sesame seeds, and nuts. Add the brown sugar, water, oil, honey, salt, cinnamon, and vanilla. Stir well. Spread in a shallow pan. Bake at 350°F for 15 minutes. Stir again. Continue baking until golden brown, about 20 more minutes. Cool. If you don't plan to use the granola within a week, store it in the refrigerator.

• • • • • • • • •

Paul Charlton of Ellensburg, Washington, was introduced to climbing by a core group of "old guard" Cascade climbers. Despite the wisdom of his mentors, Paul still had to make most of their mistakes for himself, which he managed to do during the years he worked as a National Park Service climbing ranger at Mount Rainier National Park. Climbing and other interests have taken him all over the world, but many of his best experiences involve being with close friends in his home mountains, the Stuart Range.

"Upon hearing that I'd been asked to submit a recipe for this book, my friends' jaws dropped. 'Haven't they seen what you eat? If there's anybody who should be prevented from giving advice about food, it's you.' 'No, no' chimed in another. 'Paul's contribution could only be Rainier Rice. Simply boil water, add instant rice, serve and enjoy.'

"*They did have a point. Some people find that eating good food is key to enjoying a high quality of life. I am not one of those people. My somewhat dysfunctional taste buds have many benefits. 'Fine,' I replied. 'What should I submit for a recipe? What do you usually see me eat on climbs?' Their response was, 'Must we revisit these horrors? Oh, very well then: baked potatoes; crackers and barbecue sauce; uncooked ramen noodles; applesauce, Cheerios and Fruity Pebbles rolled in a tortilla; cold pancakes with peanut butter and jam; instant rice straight from the box; potato flakes with spaghetti sauce or barbecue sauce; yeast bars in which you forgot to dissolve the yeast before you baked the bar…'*

"*In the end, I came up with this well-tested recipe. It is excellent year round, whether as a snack on the trail or with reconstituted milk for breakfast.*"

Tom Frost

Homemade Granola

2½ cups rolled cereals (combine to taste; use oatmeal alone,
    or mix it with rolled wheat and rolled rye from health food
    stores)
¼ cup sesame seeds
¼ cup sunflower seeds
½ cup shredded or flaked coconut
¼ cup wheat germ
½ cup sliced almonds
⅛ cup date sugar or ¼ cup brown sugar
½ cup water
⅓ cup honey
⅓ cup soy or safflower oil
Brewer's yeast, lecithin granules, and whey powder (optional)

Mix dry ingredients. Stir in water, honey, and oil. Spread in shallow pan. Bake 2 hours at 225°F. Cool. For a moister granola, use more honey and oil. Eat dry or mixed with dry milk and water. If desired, to boost nutrition, add brewer's yeast, lecithin, and a little whey powder just before eating.

• • • • • • • • • •

Tom Frost and his wife, Joyce, reside in Oakdale, California. He has climbed in Yosemite and the Himalaya with Yvon Chouinard, Royal Robbins, and Sir Edmund Hillary. Tom has always carried his camera on his many great adventures on the mountains. He has partnered with Chouinard to develop climbing gear, cofounded Chimera Photographic Lighting, and started Frostworks climbing hardware. He also helped the National Park Service understand the historical significance of Yosemite's Camp 4. At age 66, Tom celebrated a fortieth-anniversary ascent of the Salathe Wall by climbing it with his son. He says, "Life is truly awesome!"

"I have made various first or second ascents of Yosemite's Big Walls—the Northwest Face of Half Dome, the Northwest Face of the Higher Cathedral Spire, and several routes on Sentinel Rock and El Capitan. I have put up new routes in the Chamonix/Mont Blanc area, in the Cordillera Blanca of Peru, and on Lotus Flower Tower in the Northwest Territories. In Nepal, in 1963, I made a first ascent of 22,340-foot Kantega with part of Sir Edmund Hillary's schoolhouse expedition; in 1970 I reached 25,000 feet as a member of the Annapurna

South Face Expedition; and in 1979 I led a filming expedition to the summit of 22,494-foot Ama Dablam in the Everest area.

"Food needs vary. On Yosemite's granite walls we used to specialize in salami, cheese, hard rolls, chocolate, gorp, and water. Water and most foods were rationed, but never gorp (no need—it is very unpalatable on a thirsty wall). At high altitudes with very little oxygen, much stress, and great energy output, you need digestible nutritious food and wide variety. My granola has kept me moving over many a trail and pass."

Chet Marler

Enchantment Granola

6 cups quick oatmeal
¾ cup wheat germ
½ cup shredded or flaked coconut
½ cup brown sugar
⅓ cup sesame or sunflower seeds
1 cup nuts (chopped walnuts, pecans, or peanuts)
½ cup vegetable oil
⅓ cup honey
1½ teaspoons vanilla

Heat oven to 350°F. Place the oatmeal in a shallow pan and toast in oven for about 10 minutes. Combine the oatmeal, wheat germ, coconut, sugar, seeds, and nuts. Add the oil, honey, and vanilla. Spread in a shallow pan. Return to the oven for 20 to 25 minutes; stir every 5 minutes to brown evenly. Cool, then stir until crumbly. Makes about 10 cups. Excellent for breakfast, with or without milk. (Chopped dry fruit can be added after mixture has cooled.)

• • • • • • • • • •

Chet Marler of Leavenworth, Washington, is a mountaineer, ski tourer, alpine skier, and kayaker. He is director of planning and environmental stewardship for the Stevens Pass Ski Resort. He and his wife, Ann, have ski toured in the Tetons and the Alaska Range. Their longest tour was twelve days in the Brooks Range of Alaska.

"One of my outdoor goals used to be to make ski runs from the summits of all the volcanic cones in Washington State. I have skied down Mount Adams and down Glacier Peak via the Sitkum Glacier. In recent years, my skiing interests have directed to more extended ski tours in the backcountry of the Cascades' eastern slope. Depending upon the terrain for the tour, I use either telemark skis or alpine touring gear. The trips are usually in March or April, and extend from three to four days to over a week.

"On backcountry trips, quickie recipes are very useful. For quick dinners, I add dehydrated grated cheddar cheese that we have prepared in advance to rice or noodles. This cheese is much tastier than purchased Parmesan cheese. For simple, nutritious meals during the summer, we take prepared rice or pasta dinners plus fresh vegetables from our garden—carrots, broccoli, onions, etc. The weight is minimal for a two- to three-day trip. These additions change a very mediocre meal to something quite satisfying."

Gary McCue

Superfast Jumbo Jet All Morning Organic Porridge

1 cup organic oat porridge, or organic quick-cook oatmeal
1 small handful organic raisins
1 small handful organic walnuts, broken into small pieces
¼ teaspoon cinnamon (organic if available)
2½ cups water
½ cup chopped organic fresh or dried fruit (optional)
Raw honey, raw sugar, or organic jam, to taste
Organic milk (or powdered milk)

At home, mix together the oats, raisins, walnuts, and cinnamon. Place the mixture in a resealable plastic bag. At camp, bring the water to boil in a saucepan. Slowly pour the oat mixture into the boiling water, stirring briskly to prevent lumping. Add the fruit. When the mixture returns to a boil, reduce heat and cook slowly, stirring constantly to keep it from burning. When the water is completely absorbed and the oats are soft, remove the saucepan from the heat. Cover, and let stand for a few minutes. Spoon into bowls. Top with a spoonful of honey, sugar, or jam. Serves 2.

• • • • • • • • • •

Gary McCue lived and worked in Nepal for nearly twenty years, where he led trekking expeditions in Tibet and the Himalaya. He is the author of *Trekking in Tibet* (The Mountaineers Books). Gary now lives on the wild west coast of Tasmania with his partner, Kathy Butler.

"When trekking in Tibet, it's necessary to bring along all of your food for the entire trek, as not much is available in the villages. The staple food on the Tibetan Plateau is tsampa. It is typically prepared by mixing a small bowlful of lightly roasted barley flour with salted butter tea, though sometimes yoghurt is used. It may also include chang, a fermented barley beer, mixed in as the liquid. Using their hands, the Tibetans deftly mix this batter into a firm ball, called pak. It is consumed dry and unaccompanied by condiments. I actually like pak, as it has a nutty (almost peanut buttery) taste, but my stomach isn't impressed if I eat more than one ball per day. It's similar to eating raw cookie dough.

"Meat is not easy to obtain while trekking, since animals are mainly slaughtered in the autumn after the Tibet trek season has ended. Vegetables are also very limited, due to the difficulty of growing them at high altitudes. Mustard greens are often available in the villages in summer, and if you're lucky you might find potatoes, turnips, or peas. If you're in the high yak pastures where the nomads live, be prepared to experience the best dairy products in the world! The thick creamy yoghurt is fantastic, and a cup of hot dri milk (the dri is the female; the yak is the male) is nearly a meal in itself, for the butterfat content is higher than cow's milk. You don't have to worry about whether the dairy products are safe to consume, since the Tibetans always boil the milk before using it."

See Gary's recipe for Real Nepali Chiyaa (Chai) on page 187.

Peter and Mell Schoening

Dudleys

Quick oats
Powdered milk
Bran buds
Fruit bits, raisins, or craisins, chopped
Almonds, slivered
Raw sugar
Fresh lemon juice
Water

At home, stir together equal quantities of oats, powdered milk, and bran buds. Stir in desired quantities of fruit bits, almonds, sugar, and lemon juice. Mix well. Store mixture in a resealable plastic bag. At camp, place desired quantity of mixture in a cup, then stir in enough hot water to achieve the desired consistency. By the time you've had a cup of coffee, your breakfast is ready to eat. The 1-cup method is to have cereal first, then drink your favorite hot beverage from the same cup.

• • • • • • • • • •

The late Peter K. (Pete) Schoening of Bothell, Washington, began mountain outings with the Boy Scouts in the late 1930s. In 1946 he began climbing "seriously." After that, Pete climbed extensively in Washington, Oregon, Wyoming, Canada, and Alaska, where he made two ascents of Mount McKinley. He was a member of the historic 1953 American attempt on K2. In 1958, Pete and Andrew J. Kauffman II made a first ascent of 26,470-foot Hidden Peak (Gasherbrum I) in the Karakoram. In 1966-1967, Pete was a member of the American Antarctic Expedition that made six first ascents in the Sentinel Range. Pete climbed Vinson Massif, Shinn, Gardner, and Long Gables. In 1974 the Soviet Sports Federation invited the American Alpine Club to send an expedition to their International Pamir Camp. Pete was leader of the first American party to climb in the Soviet Union.

"'Dudleys became one of our standard breakfasts that epitomize my 'no cook' philosophy. It became daily fare for my wife, Mell, when she visited the parks of Tasmania with an Aussie guide named Dudley. Subsequently, Dudleys became customary for several three-week-long canoe trips in Alaska. Prizes have been awarded to canoers who were able to eat Dudleys every morning. Freeze leftovers for future trips or use to make oatmeal cookies.

"We enjoy another breakfast, developed on Glacier Meadows in February, 1951.

Harvey Manning was in our Mount Olympus climbing party. During white-out conditions, we stopped at a small cabin in Hoh Valley. After we dried out in front of a nice fire, we had Chinese egg noodles and corned beef. Party member Chuck Allyn tells the story: 'The next morning we had what we dubbed "Mount Olympus 1951 Breakfast." It consisted of desired proportions of sweetened condensed milk, cocoa powder, Grape-Nuts, and raisins (or pitted prunes).' This breakfast requires no fire, which gave an early start to our climbing day."

Anni Grasegger

Emperor's Scrambled Pancakes

1 cup sifted all-purpose flour
1 tablespoon sugar
¼ teaspoon salt
4 eggs, beaten
1 cup milk (reconstituted dry)
½ cup (¼-pound stick) butter (NOT margarine)
Sugar, to taste

Combine flour, sugar, and salt in a bowl or saucepan. Make a well in center of dry ingredients, and add the eggs and milk. Beat until batter is smooth. In a frying pan, melt butter and add the batter all at once, and cook until lightly browned on bottom. Turn over with a spatula, as for scrambled eggs—the pancake will break into pieces. Continue to cook until the other side is lightly browned but the pancake is still moist. Serve sprinkled with sugar. It is delicious with applesauce on the side and a cup of hot, Italian-style, orange-flavored instant coffee beverage. The German name for these pancakes is *Kaiser Schmarren*. Serves 2.

• • • • • • • • • •

Anni Grasegger of Seattle, Washington, was born and grew up in Garmisch-Partenkirchen in the foothills of the Bavarian Alps. In 2003, at the age of 78, she reports that "nature is in her soul," and she is still called to the hills, although not the steep ones. She is never without her trusty old Rolleiflex and Pentax cameras.

"I learned to ski in kindergarten, as did all my friends. I climbed Germany's highest mountain, the 9700-foot Zugspitze, for the first time when I was eleven. Since then, I have been in love with the outdoors. In 1953, after doing photographic work for fourteen years in my hometown, I emigrated to Seattle, where I am a lab technician specializing in color reproduction. Photography—and discovering the infinite beauty of the Pacific Northwest on foot and with my camera—are my main hobbies.

"I particularly enjoy hiking in the Cascades. My favorite spot is Snow Lake, north of Snoqualmie Pass, as it reminds me so much of the lakes I know in the Bavarian Alps. I return fairly often to Bavaria. In the Bavarian Alps hiking means having, at all times, a hütte (mountain lodge) as home base for shelter and meals. Like everywhere else, soups are the basic dishes. Lentil soup and green pea soup, with one of the many delicious Bavarian sausages, are favorites. Here, Bavarian

sausage can be replaced by cocktail sausages available in glass jars. A popular trail snack in Germany is called studentenfutter—named after university students who had to put together an inexpensive and readily available trail food. Usual ingredients are nuts, raisins, and chocolate, with the addition of dried fruits such as apples, pears, or peaches."

William Lokey

Mountain McMuffins

2-ounce can freeze-dried ham
Freeze-dried eggs equal to 2 servings
¼ cup margarine, or to taste
1 package (0.9 ounce to 1.25 ounce) hollandaise sauce mix
2 English muffins (or other substitute)
4 ounces cheese, sliced thick
Salt and pepper, to taste

Reconstitute ham and eggs as directed on packages. Add the ham to the eggs. Melt 2 to 3 tablespoons of margarine in a frying pan over low heat. Add egg mixture. Gently stir till eggs are no longer runny. In a separate pot, prepare hollandaise sauce according to package directions. Toast muffins over the stove. Spread with margarine. Place 2 halves of a muffin in a heated cup or bowl. Pile the egg mixture on top of the muffins. Top with cheese, and cover completely with hollandaise sauce. Repeat with second muffin. Season with salt and pepper. Serves 2.

• • • • • • • • • •

William (Bill) Lokey of Tacoma, Washington, works for the Federal Emergency Management Agency (FEMA). He has climbed extensively in the Pacific Northwest, Alaska, Mexico, France, Africa, New Zealand, the Arctic, and the Antarctic. While Bill was working for the United States Antarctic Research Program, he spent three winters in the Antarctic at various stations. In 1974 he made an around-the-world snowshoe trek, a feat accomplished by snowshoeing in a small circle around the South Pole at a latitude of approximately 09° 59' 59"! He spent six summers on the Juneau Icefield in southeast Alaska. In addition to thirty-six ascents of Mount Rainier, Bill has climbed new routes on Alaska's Mount Hubbard (1973) and Mount Vancouver (1976). In April 1980, he climbed Mount McKinley via Pioneer Ridge, and in 1987, he climbed Mount Waddington, the highest point in British Columbia.

"Sometimes, life on the Juneau Icefield was a dog's life. In May 1971, I led a small group that snowshoed ten miles of trail and glacier from Juneau to the Arctic Sciences Institute's main camp at about 3500 feet. We dug the snow away from the door, started our weather observations, and performed the annual spring housecleaning and fix-up that preceded the arrival of students and staff of the Juneau Icefield Research Project.

"The previous fall, a big box of unlabeled cans that had collected over the years had been stashed. As the camp is stocked by helicopter and the cost of supplies is high, nothing is wasted. So I made it a camp rule that we had to eat the contents of four of the unlabeled cans a day till all were gone. Some were good; most weren't bad; but the hash (beef or corned beef) seemed to be of low quality and hadn't been improved by a winter of freezing and thawing. But we ate it. A few weeks later, a staff member showed up inquiring about the eight cans of dog food he had left in the storage box the year before. It seemed that his constant companion, a husky, was hungry."

June Fleming

Protein Power Muffins

1 cup all-purpose flour
½ cup whole-wheat flour
½ cup soy flour
¼ cup granulated sugar
2 teaspoons pumpkin pie
  spice
2 teaspoons baking soda
½ teaspoon salt
3 eggs
¼ cup vegetable oil

½ cup applesauce
2 cups carrots or zucchini,
  grated
½ cup walnuts, chopped
½ cup raisins
½ cup flaked or shredded
  coconut
½ cup canned crushed
  pineapple, undrained

In a large bowl combine the flours, sugar, pumpkin pie spice, baking soda, and salt. In a small bowl, beat the eggs, then add the oil and applesauce. Stir the wet ingredients into the dry ingredients. Fold in the carrots (or zucchini), walnuts, raisins, coconut, and pineapple. Pour the batter into greased muffin tins (⅔ full). Bake at 350°F for 25 to 30 minutes, or until tops of muffins spring back when touched lightly. Makes 24 muffins.

• • • • • • • • • •

June Fleming of Portland, Oregon, has taught outdoor skills for thirty years. These include backpacking, snow camping, preparing trail foods, using a map and compass, winter safety, and routefinding on snow. Her books include *The Well-Fed Backpacker* (Vintage Books) and *Staying Found: the Complete Map and Compass Handbook* (The Mountaineers Books).

"Muffins ride well in a cook kit and seem luxurious on the trail, as well as being nutritious and tasty. Muffin batter can also be baked in loaf form for easier packing. A slice adds a welcome energy boost. Waking up to a summer rain or a blizzard in snow camp, muffins and dried fruit provide a fast and easy breakfast in bed.

"A lesson learned early in my backcountry years has smoothed out countless trips. ALWAYS pack many foods that require no cooking! When you are wiped out from the day's efforts, or there isn't enough daylight, time, or dry weather for cooking…bring out the quick breads, turkey jerky, fruit leather, trail mix, energy bars, and trail shakes."

See June's recipes for S'Mores Bars, page 150, Trail-Happy Salad, page 81, and Trail Coffees, page 160.

Chris Bonington

Peach Pancakes

2 cups pancake mix (commercial or homemade)
Water or milk to make batter of desired consistency
1 fresh peach
Butter or other shortening
Natural yogurt (optional)
Maple syrup (optional)

Prepare batter. Add the peeled and thinly sliced peach. Fry the pancakes in shortening till both sides are golden brown. Serve rolled up with yogurt, topped with maple syrup, if desired. Serves 2.

● ● ● ● ● ● ● ● ● ●

Christian (Chris) Bonington, who lives near Wigton in Cumbria, England, is most noted for his expedition planning and classic ascents of the world's highest peaks. Some notable achievements are the South Face of Annapurna, the Southwest Face of Everest, the Ogre, the West Summit of Shivling, and the West Peak of Menlungtse. Chris has received many awards, including knighthood in 1996. In addition to collaborating on a number of films, he has authored fifteen books, including *Boundless Horizons, The Autobiography of Chris Bonington* (The Mountaineers Books), and *Chris Bonington's Everest* (International Marine/Ragged Mountain Press).

"Peach Pancakes were a delicacy that my wife, Wendy, and I used to cheer ourselves up with at breakfast one summer when we camped for several weeks near Leysin, Switzerland—most of the time in the rain.

"The importance of food on high-mountain expeditions is emphasized by Mike Thompson in his appendix on food in Annapurna South Face*: 'Food was the consuming passion and obsession of the expedition.... The High Altitude rations, due to the rigours of the Face and the effects of altitude, were subjected to a much tougher testing than food at Base Camp.... Some items became popular as new ways of cooking them were devised. At first the Christmas Pudding did not get eaten, except by Tom Frost who regularly ate two at a sitting, but Christmas Pudding Boysen—thinly sliced, fried, drenched in whisky and served en flambante with cream—was universally appreciated (except by Frost . . .). Christmas Pudding Bonington—a thin gruel made by stewing the pudding with melted snow, sugar and whisky—was really only appreciated by the inventor, who nevertheless forced it upon anyone unfortunate enough to share his tent . . . . Far from being too exhausted even to light the Primus, we found that the cooking of long and elaborate meals was the main cultural activity of high-altitude life. . . . '"

*Annapurna South Face by Chris Bonington, copyright 1971 by the Mount Everest Foundation Annapurna South Face Expedition 1970. Used with permission of McGraw-Hill Book Co.

Bob Swenson

Sourdough Hotcakes

1 cup sourdough starter
2½ cups flour
2 cups warm water
1 egg (or equivalent in reconstituted dried egg)
¼ cup dry milk
2 tablespoons vegetable oil or melted bacon fat
1 cup mountain blueberries or presoaked dry applesauce
   (optional)
2 tablespoons sugar
1 teaspoon salt
1 teaspoon baking soda
Butter, margarine, or oil for frying
Syrup (or, berries or applesauce)

Well before your trip, obtain the sourdough starter (see recipe on next page). At camp, after deciding there will be time the next morning for sourdough pancakes, mix the starter with the flour and warm water. This batter should be placed overnight in a covered pot, in a warm protected part of the tent. Next morning, put 1 cup of this batter into your starter jar to save for next time. To the remaining batter add egg, milk, oil or melted bacon fat, fruit (if any), sugar, salt, and baking soda. Fry hotcakes in butter, margarine, or oil, and serve with syrup. The ultimate syrup is made by cooking copious amounts of blueberries or huckleberries with sugar the night before and reheating in the morning. You can also make a syrup using dried applesauce, sugar, and a pinch of cinnamon. Serves 2 to 3.

• • • • • • • • • •

Bob Swenson of Bellevue, Washington, started climbing in the mid-1950s when he lived in Yakima. He has made numerous ascents in the Cascades and Olympics and climbed in the Tetons of Wyoming and the Sawtooths of Idaho. For many years he was active in mountain rescue work. Today he is encouraged by the dedicated folks who now carry the mountain rescue mantle.

"Sourdough hotcakes are a delight in the mountains, but require special effort. Transport the cup of starter in a pint-size jar with a tight lid, well sealed in a double plastic sack. Otherwise, it may expand and seek every corner of your pack till you have to wring it out of your socks to have enough for the morrow. You must also nurture the batter carefully overnight, being sure to issue an

'under pain of death' warning to those who might make late night visits and kick the pot."

Sourdough starter: Starter is basically a combination of milk and flour kept warm till a special bacterial reaction occurs. It can be made by keeping a cup of raw milk warm for 24 hours, stirring in a cup of flour, and letting the mixture stand in an uncovered crock or glass jar at about 80°F for 2 to 5 days, till it turns sour and bubbly. However, this doesn't always work. It is more reliable to buy starter mix at a specialty food shop. And the best way, if it can be done, is to get starter from a friend. At home, between uses, refrigerate or freeze the stuff.

Allen Steck

Austrian Pancakes (*Palaschinken* or *Schmarren*)

1 cup flour
1 cup liquid milk
2 eggs (fresh or equivalent dried)
¼ cup sugar
1 tablespoon salt
Butter
Berries if available

Mix together all the ingredients except the butter and berries. A tablespoon of salt sounds like a lot, but a salty-sweet taste is what you are after in this recipe. Heat a frying pan, and when it is hot add a pat of butter to melt. Pour in enough batter to make the desired size of pancake. After it browns on one side, turn the cake with a spatula. Fried plain in butter, these are called *palaschinken* ("pancakes" in Austrian dialect). However, after they are fried on one side, they are often cut into small pieces and totally cooked to a golden brown. Then they are called *schmarren* and are usually served with a very tart fresh fruit, such as blueberries or blackberries. Austrians use *preisselbeeren*, European berries related to huckleberries. Serves 2 to 4.

* * * * * * * * * *

Allen Steck of Berkeley, California, is a retired writer, photographer, trekking consultant, and longtime climber. In the late 1940s and early 1950s he made many difficult rock ascents in Yosemite and the Dolomites. In the 1950s and 1960s he made the first ascent of the North Face of Mount Waddington, the highest peak in British Columbia; was on the first ascent of the East Peak of Huandoy in Peru; and climbed the Hummingbird Ridge of Mount Logan, a new route. Allen's last major expedition was in 1976, when he helped the Pakistan Alpine Club make the first ascent of Paiju Peak in Pakistan.

Allen is founder and coeditor of *Ascent*, a mountaineering publication of the Sierra Club. He is also the author of *Ascent: The Climbing Experience in Word and Image* (with coauthors Steve Roper and David Harris; The American Alpine Club) and *Fifty Classic Climbs of North America* (with coauthor Steve Roper; Sierra Club Books).

"My climbing efforts have not been without comic relief. In the 1950s, the late Willi Unsoeld and I made an attempt on the East Buttress of El Capitan in

Yosemite. We were retreating at dusk and chose a direct way down the cliff—not the route of ascent. One of the rappels landed us in a bay tree that grew horizontally out of the sheer cliff, with no ledge. The thing was 'in heat'—with lots of pollen. I was overcome with sneezing during our entire time in that tree. Have you ever tried to rappel entirely from a tree, and in the dark? I finally set the rappel, only to discover when I put my weight on the rope that I had placed the rope over Willi's leg as well as around the tree trunk. There was much laughter and pain that night."

Gary Lyon

Igloo Creek French Toast

4 slices bread
Freeze-dried or dried scrambled egg mix for 2 servings
Dry milk, about half the amount of dried egg mix
Warm water
Butter (optional)
Bacon bar (optional)
Syrup (use a powdered or freeze-dried mix, or simply boil
    brown sugar with a little water)

At home, cut bread slices into 1-inch squares, and set them out until they are stale. Store bread in a resealable plastic bag. At camp, mix dried eggs and dry milk together in another resealable plastic bag, and add enough warm water to make a slightly thick liquid. Dunk bread pieces into the egg-milk mixture and brown in a frying pan (a nonstick coated pan works well; or fry in a little butter). Sprinkle browned bread squares with the crumbled bacon bar, add butter if you have it, and serve with warm syrup. This makes a good 1-pan meal. Serve with a hot drink such as coffee, cocoa, or orange-flavored instant coffee beverage. Serves 2.

• • • • • • • • • •

Gary Lyon is a wildlife artist who lives in Homer, Alaska.

"I came to Alaska in the early 1970s to find wilderness, wild animals, and few cities. Alaska has all that I looked for. I make my living by painting in watercolors and other media. My favorite subjects are animals in their natural wild settings.

"For me, backpacking is probably the most rewarding way of experiencing the wilderness. I have hiked on the Kenai Peninsula, in the Wrangell Mountains northeast of Anchorage, in the Chugach Mountains in southern Alaska east of Anchorage, in Mount McKinley (now Denali) National Park, and in other remote areas. The national park is the best place to see wildlife: ptarmigan, golden eagles, caribou, moose—and grizzly bears, which cannot be seen in many other places.

"Once while backpacking above timberline (grassline?) in the Chugach Mountains, my companion and I were returning to camp after a grueling all-day trek. The wind was so strong that we had to lie down and wait for a lull, then run for 20 to 50 yards till the wind picked up. When we got to camp—the camp was

gone! All that remained was our stove and the front tent peg with its line blowing in the wind. We set out down a creek bed for lower ground and picked up some of our belongings as we went. Wet sleeping bags had been blown a mile. Many things were never found. Of our food, only cheese, sausage, and a few crackers survived. Freeze-dried food sacks were torn, the contents soaked and useless. We learned that in backpacking, the unexpected always happens. One should carry some durable food for that inevitable adventure."

John Rugge

Adirondack Sweet Rolls

2 cups biscuit mix
½ cup sugar
⅔ cup water (approximate)
1 teaspoon cinnamon
4 to 6 tablespoons margarine
½ cup raisins—or better yet, fresh berries in season (blueberries, wild strawberries, raspberries, etc.)
½ cup powdered (icing) sugar
Boiling water

Combine biscuit mix with ¼ cup of the sugar. Add enough water to make a firm dough. Pat out an inch or less thick. Cover dough with remaining ¼ cup sugar, cinnamon, a couple of tablespoons melted margarine, and fruit. Cut dough into strips, and roll into cylinders (or roll up the whole slab, and slice into cylinders ¾ to 1 inch thick). Melt some margarine in a frying pan, carefully lay the rounds of sweet rolls in the pan, cover, and cook over low heat. Meanwhile, mix the powdered sugar with 2 tablespoons melted margarine, add boiling water a few drops at a time, and stir until icing reaches desired creamy consistency. Spread or drizzle it over the rolls when they are ready to serve. Serves 2 to 4.

· · · · · · · · · ·

John Rugge, M.D., lives in Queensbury, New York. He is a canoeist, and with James West Davidson is coauthor of *The Complete Wilderness Paddler* (Vintage). The book is a guide to canoeing and expedition technique, and it tells the story of a trip down the Moisie River in Labrador and Quebec. John and James also coauthored *Great Heart* (Kodansha International), a narrative history of the Hubbard and Wallace expedition of 1903 and 1904 in Labrador.

John practices medicine and founded the Hudson Headwaters Health Network, a system of community health centers in the Glens Falls/Lake George/Adirondacks region. He still canoes in the Adirondacks.

"My first long canoe trip was when I was eleven—a ten-day excursion through the Adirondacks, on which my father came up with blueberry sweet rolls. I don't remember the rolls very well, but I do remember the Boy Scouts who camped near us that morning. They each had a bowl of crushed cornflakes for breakfast. My father invited a couple of them over to share our bounty. When

they returned to their own camp, we overheard one of them tell the others, 'Hey, that kid over there, he's got his own guide!'

"Another treat in the wilderness that no one seems to think of is popcorn. The cooking technique is about the same as the one you use at home, but use a frying pan with a cover; this avoids the nuisance of burning your cooking pot. Preheat margarine in the frying pan over medium-high heat. Put in a couple of test kernels to help avoid scorching the corn. When it is popped, add salt to taste. Lean back against a tree—and if the night is right, catch the aurora borealis late show."

Charles D. Hessey

Lyman Lake Hotcakes

1 cup flour
⅔ cup buckwheat pancake mix
2 teaspoons baking powder
3 teaspoons sugar
½ teaspoon salt
Wheat germ, to taste (optional)
1½ cups milk (more or less for thinner or thicker batter)
1 to 2 tablespoons vegetable oil or melted shortening
1 egg (optional)
Butter, margarine, or oil for frying
Syrup (preferably made with wild blueberries, sugar, and
    water)

At home, sift together flour, pancake mix, baking powder, sugar, and salt 5 times. Add wheat germ. Pack in a resealable plastic bag. At camp, stir oil or melted shortening and egg into dry mix. Fry hotcakes on a greased skillet. Serves 2. The best syrup is made from wild blueberries or huckleberries cooked with sugar and water and served hot. Or, try Steve Markoskie's Oregon Grape Syrup, page 174.

• • • • • • • • • •

Charles D. (Chuck) Hessey of Naches, Washington, was camping, fishing, backpacking, and skiing in the North Cascades before World War II. After the war he made numerous cross-country ski treks from Holden, west of Lake Chelan, to a shelter cabin eight miles away at Lyman Lake (now in the Glacier Peak Wilderness Area). Chuck spent long periods at the cabin and left a log of weather observations and philosophy, which inspired those at the mining camp above Holden to give him the title "The Lyman Lake Philosopher." Chuck and his wife, Marion, have contributed much toward preserving the North Cascades Wilderness, in part through Chuck's wildlife films.

"During my service with the United States Army in India, I had the experience—rare for an American—of skiing in the Vale of Kashmir. I had joined the Ski Club of India and was able to enjoy a ten-day ski outing at the Killenmarg Hut at Gulmarg, then a British Air Force rest camp at over 10,000 feet elevation on the slopes of Mount Apharwat. It was wonderful for a mountain-starved soldier from the Pacific Northwest. Conditions were similar to winter conditions on North Star Mountain near Lyman Lake. But there were some differences.

"We were taken to the resort by lorry, with our personal possessions in dunnage bags. Our food supply was largely C rations, supplemented by tea, eggs, and brown sugar from a local bazaar. We rented boots and skis in Srinagar. From there we were transported by truck to the base of Apharwat. There we hired porters, who were barefoot except for sandals, to carry our gear to Killenmarg. They were the Indian version of a ski lift—supplemented by donkeys. Aided by our porters, we rode the donkeys up and skied down!"

Energizing Snacks, Breads, and Lunches

I t is generally agreed that snacking during short breaks throughout the day is the best way to keep your muscles going. But you'll find differing views when it comes to the best choice of snack food. To some, it's something you can grab out of your pocket and munch on the trail. Others like to sit down and eat, for a longer break.

In the following pages you will find a vast selection of snacks, including energy nuggets and bars, tasty gorps, sturdy breads, bagels, rich and nutty fruit breads, luscious coffee cakes, and even a classic pemmican.

Some of the breads, like bannock and flat bread, can be made at breakfast, to eat later. Combine those with a bit of honey, nut butter, or jam, and you've got a meal.

If it's a zesty salad you crave, turn to "Savory Salads," beginning on page 79.

Finally, for a warm lunch, there are lots of great options in the "Celebrate the Day Dinners" chapter, beginning on page 87.

Give these action-packed trail treats a try. Take a break, enjoy the scenery, and recharge your internal battery!

Claudia Pearson

Katie's No-Bake Energy Nuggets

½ cup sunflower seeds and/or chopped nuts
1 cup raisins, craisins, or small pieces dried fruit
½ cup hydrated granola (combine with ½ cup warm water to
    hydrate granola), or ½ cup cooked brown/white rice
½ cup nut butter (peanut, almond, or cashew)
½ cup powdered milk
½ cup honey
1 cup dried regular or instant oatmeal
1 teaspoon cinnamon
Vanilla (a few drops)
¼ to ½ cup whole-wheat flour

Stir together all ingredients except the flour. The mixture will be sticky. Gradually add the flour until the mixture becomes less sticky. Let set in a cool place (e.g. on the snow, under a shaded tree, or in or near a stream) for 15 to 20 minutes, or until the ingredients bind together. Pinch off small amounts and roll into 2-inch nuggets. Store in a sealed container or resealable plastic bag, and keep cool. These are very dense, one makes for a filling snack. Eat within 2 days. Makes 30 bite-sized nuggets.

● ● ● ● ● ● ● ● ● ●

Katie Wewer is an avid backcountry enthusiast. She conducted nutrient analyses of each recipe in the 2004 edition of *NOLS Cookery*. She recently completed the Coordinated Master's Degree Program at the University of Utah, College of Health, with a degree in Foods and Nutrition.

    Claudia Pearson has worked as the Rations Manager for the National Outdoor Leadership School (NOLS) Rocky Mountain since May 1978, after graduating from the University of Colorado. She has been directly involved in the second through the fifth edition revisions of the *NOLS Cookery* books. Claudia lives in a log cabin on a few acres near Lander, Wyoming. For many years Claudia's passion has been horses. She re-trains young horses off the track as dressage and jumping prospects, and she teaches English riding. Claudia also rides a great deal in the mountains around Lander and has done several pack trips using horses.

See Claudia's recipe for Donna's Gado-Gado Spaghetti, page 114, and Mary's Fantastic Bulgur Pilaf, page 107.

Recipe reprinted with permission from *NOLS Cookery,* fifth edition, 2004.

Craig Romano and Heather Scott

Sicilian Bagels

¼ cup raw, unhulled sesame seeds
1 15-ounce can garbanzo beans, drained and liquid reserved
3 tablespoons lemon juice
2 tablespoons olive oil
1 clove garlic (or more to taste)
4 large slices roasted red peppers
Hot pepper sauce, to taste
Salt and pepper, to taste
Sun-dried tomatoes, to taste
6 to 8 bagels (onion or garlic are best)

At home, toast the sesame seeds in a frying pan over medium heat until golden brown (about 5 minutes). Place toasted seeds in a blender. Add the garbanzo beans, 6 tablespoons of their liquid, garlic, red peppers, lemon juice, olive oil, hot pepper sauce, salt, and pepper. Blend until smooth and creamy, adding more garbanzo bean liquid if necessary. Taste and adjust the seasonings or add oil to your liking. Spread the mixture in a thin layer on a dehydrator tray. Dehydrate until mixture is visibly dried and crumbly. In a clean, dry blender, pulse the dried mixture until it resembles crumbs. Store in an airtight container. At camp, for each person, place a sixth or an eighth of the dried mixture in a bowl. Add chopped sun-dried tomatoes. Slowly pour boiling water over the mixture, stirring until desired consistency is reached. Cover the bowls and let stand for 5 minutes. Add more water if necessary. Spread on bagels. Serves 6 to 8 (¼ cup each, reconstituted).

Enjoy for lunch or eat for a high-powered breakfast.

• • • • • • • • • •

Craig Romano and Heather Scott lead hiking tours in the mountains of Europe for Walking Softly Adventures. They have traveled extensively, covering ground from Argentina to Alaska, Slovenia to Indonesia. Craig and Heather live in Seattle, Washington, where he is an outdoor writer and she is enrolled in Bastyr University's Nutrition Program.

"We love to eat well when we travel. We often rate our favorite places in the world by how good the fare is there. No surprise then that Italy ranks supreme, especially the south and Sicily. For treats from the sea, you can't beat Japan. Argentina by far has the best beef. The Koreans know how to make a mean

barbecue, and the Brazilians barbecue everything—chicken hearts anyone? Half the fun of traveling is sampling the culinary delights of the world.

"When we're home in North America, our taste buds don't take a vacation. Out in the backcountry after a grueling day on the trail, we don't yearn for peanut butter and jelly and prefab dehydrated meals. We crave flavor, spices, and good and tasty dishes that are easy to prepare.

"Raisins and peanuts are fine, but we prefer our gorp: garlic, olives, and roasted peppers. Home dehydrators make it possible to bypass the bland (and often expensive) backcountry foods that are passed off as meals. You can make some mighty tasty pastes, spreads, and dishes with those things. Now if we could dehydrate an empanada or an anchovy, we'd really be cooking."

Jeff Renner

Snow Cake

⅔ stick (5 tablespoons) butter
⅓ cup honey
⅔ cup coarsely chopped cranberries
2 teaspoons lemon juice
1 egg, beaten
1 cup flour
1 teaspoon baking powder
⅓ teaspoon salt
⅓ cup powdered milk
1 teaspoon powdered ginger
⅔ teaspoon ground nutmeg
⅔ teaspoon ground cardamom (or clove)
⅔ cup chopped dates
⅔ cup chopped nuts
⅔ cup chopped apricots
1 cup raisins

Melt butter in small saucepan. Slowly stir in the honey until it is completely incorporated into the butter. Place the cranberries in a small bowl. Stir in the lemon juice and egg, and then add the butter/honey mixture. In a large bowl, mix together the flour, baking powder, salt, powdered milk, ginger, nutmeg, cardamom, dates, nuts, apricots, and raisins. Stir in the cranberry mixture. Pour the mixture into a greased loaf pan (about 8½ x 4½ x 2½-inch). Bake at 325°F for 1½ to 2 hours. Exact baking time depends upon your oven. Begin testing for doneness after the first hour with a toothpick or knife. Repeat every 10 minutes or so until it comes out clean. Cool completely. Slice and wrap individual slices in plastic wrap. Use a food processor to reduce prep time!

• • • • • • • • •

Jeff Renner is chief meteorologist at KING-TV in Seattle, Washington, and is the author of *Lightning Strikes: Staying Safe Under Stormy Skies* (The Mountaineers Books) and *Northwest Marine Weather* (The Mountaineers Books) and a contributing author to *Mountaineering: Freedom of the Hills* (The Mountaineers Books). He's a skier, climber, and snowshoer who enjoys snow camping in the Cascades of Washington.

"Fruitcake is a much maligned food, and often rightly so. Generally it's as dense as a hockey puck with a flavor resembling envelope glue. Much to my

amazement, this cake not only tastes great, but also quickly stokes the internal fires after a long day of skiing, snowshoeing, and snow cave building. It's become a mandatory menu item for my backcountry snow camping trips.

"There are two hazards related to this cake. First, I often skijor with our Siberian husky, Kiana. One year I had led a Boy Scout troop on an outing near Snoqualmie Pass. Some of the boys hadn't been very neat while eating this cake, and crumbs had fallen into the snow around their snow cave. Kiana's keen sense of smell led her to begin digging in the snow for some morsels. Seconds later, I heard shouts loud enough to trigger an avalanche. Turning, I noticed her disappear into what was now a pit filled with thrashing arms, legs, and one furry creature. Much to the surprise of the Scouts inside, Kiana had dug her way through the roof of their snow cave! The second hazard relates to the high caloric content of this recipe. It's great when you're working hard in a cold environment, but will leave you with the contours of a snowman if you snack on it too much at home!"

See Jeff's recipe for Trail Cider, page 161.

David Mahre

High-Energy Fruit Bars

¼ pound (½ cup) butter or margarine
4 medium eggs, well beaten
1 cup sifted flour
½ teaspoon baking powder
1 teaspoon salt
1¾ cups sugar
2 cups dates, pitted and chopped
2 cups glazed (or candied) fruit
2½ cups chopped walnuts

Melt butter and cool slightly. Add to well-beaten eggs. Sift together flour, baking powder, salt, and sugar, and add to the egg/shortening mixture. Mix together fruits and nuts, and stir into batter. Spread in 2 greased 9 x 9-inch square baking pans. Bake 30 minutes at 350°F. Cool, cut into bars, and wrap individually in plastic wrap.

. . . .

David "Spike" Mahre of Yakima, Washington, is a long-time guide and ski adventurer. For many years he and his wife, Mary, and their children lived at the White Pass ski area southeast of Mount Rainier National Park, where he worked in one capacity or another. Dave has climbed for many years. He put up new routes on the north sides of Stuart, Adams, Little Tahoma, and Rainier—particularly around the Willis Wall area. On Mount McKinley, Dave learned that, at age 69, he was the oldest active guide to summit the mountain. He continues to climb, ski, and guide occasional parties.

"I'll never forget an episode on the side of Everest, where we camped at about 23,400 feet. It was an awesome and breathtaking sight: an expedition member, unroped, was chasing a roll of toilet paper he'd dropped on the way to the latrine. Sliding and about to lose his balance on a 60-degree slope above a crevasse, he saved himself by jamming a cup in the side of the mountain. The toilet paper kept going.

"Other favorite memories in the outdoors include mountain rescues all over the Cascades. During my years doing mountain rescue, I pioneered the use of hard hats and helped improve ice axes, the rigid crampons used for climbing, and rescue techniques. I will always treasure the lifelong friendships that were forged through years of rescues.

"Regarding food, I always relied on my buddies or my wife, Mary, to feed me. Mary often includes High-Energy Fruit Bars in my food supply. Sometimes, before I climb, I stop at a deli and buy fried chicken. I top off the meal with fruit bars and something hot to drink like Russian Tea or Sherpa Grog."

Dave's daughters, Ruth Mahre and Kathee Forman, also contributed recipes to this volume. See pages 60, 62, 125, and 152. Russian Tea is on page 163, and Sherpa Grog is on page 165.

Anne LaBastille

Quick Health Bread

2½ cups whole-wheat flour
½ teaspoon cinnamon
¼ teaspoon salt
1 teaspoon baking soda
1 egg
½ cup molasses
¼ cup dark brown sugar or
   honey

¼ cup safflower oil
⅔ cup buttermilk or yogurt
Grated orange or lemon
   peel, citron, dates,
   raisins, or nuts,
   to taste

Combine flour, cinnamon, salt, and soda. Add the remaining ingredients, and mix. Pour into a greased 8½ x 4½ x 2½-inch loaf pan and bake approximately 50 minutes at 375°F. Test for doneness with a toothpick or pine needle. Cool the loaf. Eat, or wrap and store.

• • • • • • • • • •

Anne LaBastille of New York State is one of the most experienced outdoorswomen in the eastern United States. An author, biologist, conservationist, and explorer, she has hiked and camped in the Adirondacks for more than twenty-five years and is an active licensed wilderness guide. She took her Ph.D. in wildlife ecology at Cornell University. Research and outdoor interests have taken her to Central America, the Caribbean Islands, the Amazon basin, and Europe.

Some years ago Anne acquired 30 acres on the shore of a lake in New York's Adirondack Park. In her book *Woodswoman* (E.P. Dutton), she describes her experiences there building a small log cabin studio, which can be reached only by foot, boat, canoe, or snowshoe. She relates how she splits her own wood and in winter chops a hole in the lake ice to get water. In her tenth and latest book, *Woodswoman IV* (West of the Wind, 2003), Anne describes her thriving book business, her beloved dogs, a frightening two-mile walk over unsafe ice in February, and mystical encounters with hummingbirds and other wildlife. She counsels women everywhere to be independent, fit, and to work to save the planet.

"I like to carry a heavy, wholesome, sweet health bread. It goes well alone, or with cheese, peanut butter, and jelly. I first learned to depend on bread when hiking with European students in the Black Forest of Germany. Bread was the mainstay of most meals, with soup, cheese, sausages, and tea."

Chris Townsend

Ooey-Gooey Flapjacks

¼ cup oats (not instant or quick-cook)
¼ cup wheat flour
⅓ cup cornflakes
½ cup butter or margarine
½ cup sugar
1 generous tablespoon syrup (golden syrup is ideal, maple for
special taste, corn syrup if necessary)

Mix together the oats, flour, and cornflakes. Melt together the butter, sugar, and syrup. Stir together wet and dry ingredients. Spread in a baking pan. Bake for 20 minutes at 375°F. Cool, and cut into bars. Cool completely and wrap individually in plastic wrap.

● ● ● ● ● ● ● ● ● ●

Chris Townsend is the author of many outdoor books, including *The Advanced Backpacker: A Handbook of Year Round, Long-Distance Hiking* (Ragged Mountain Press). A passionate wilderness hiker and skier, he has hiked the Pacific Crest Trail, the Continental Divide Trail, the Arizona Trail, the length of the Canadian Rockies, and the length of the Yukon Territory. In addition, Chris has ski toured in Greenland, Spitsbergen, Lapland, the Yukon, and the Sierra Nevada. He lives in Scotland.

"This is a British high-energy sweet cookie. The recipe and the name were given to me many years ago—by whom, I have forgotten—though I still have it tucked away in an old cookbook. There are many possible variations. Raisins and nuts can be added. Honey can be used instead of the sugar or syrup. More oats and less, or no flour or cornflakes make a coarser flapjack. Muesli can be used instead of the dry ingredients, for a flapjack that is more like a granola bar. I much prefer homemade flapjacks to any commercial energy bar."

See Chris's recipe for Scandinavian Macaroni, page 108 and Ski Tour Chili Rice, page 112.

Herb and Jan Conn

Apple Logan Bread

1½ cups water
1¾ cups sugar
2 cups applesauce
½ cup molasses
⅔ cup honey
2 cups shortening
7 to 8 cups (2 pounds) whole wheat flour
2⅔ cups white flour
⅔ cup dry milk
1 teaspoon baking powder
2 teaspoons baking soda
1 teaspoon salt
1 generous teaspoon ground cloves
1 generous teaspoon ground nutmeg

Combine water, sugar, applesauce, molasses, honey, and shortening. Bring mixture to a boil. Mix the dry ingredients thoroughly, then stir into the liquid. Pour dough into greased loaf pans, filling pans about ⅔ full. Bake at 300°F for about 1 hour. Cool, remove from pans, wrap in foil, and store in refrigerator.

• • • • • • • • •

Herb and Jan Conn, who live near Custer, South Dakota, are a husband-and-wife climbing and caving team of long standing. They were pioneer rock climbers in the Washington, D.C., area in the early 1940s. They have made various ascents in the Tetons and elsewhere. Herb was on the first ascent in 1949 of Agathlan in Monument Valley, Arizona, and in 1950 he was in a party that made a new route on Devils Tower, Wyoming.

Herb and Jan moved to the Black Hills of South Dakota in 1949. Between then and 1960 they put up 215 first ascents in this popular climbing mecca. They also surveyed and mapped extensively in the region and over the years kept detailed records of climbing activities. Herb wrote the area's first climbing guide, a mimeographed treatise entitled "Rock Climbs in the Needles, Black Hills of South Dakota." The Conns' records and recollections were the basis of a 1971 guidebook written by Bob Kamps. Bob dedicated his book, *A Climber's Guide to the Needles in the Black Hills of South Dakota* (American Alpine Club), to Herb and Jan. In 1983 Paul Piana wrote a more extensive guide to the area, *Touch the Sky: The Needles in the*

Black Hills of South Dakota (The American Alpine Club). Today Herb and Jan have "returned to the surface" to hike to scenic summits, rather than undertake other challenging climbs.

"We climbed—mostly in the Needles of the Black Hills—until we degenerated into cave exploring. The first cave we took a serious interest in was Jewel Cave (in Jewel Cave National Monument). We spent twenty-two years trying without success to find the end of it, and we have mapped approximately sixty-six miles of underground passages. The cave's mapping continues under the leadership of Mike Wiles. Anyone curious to know more about the exploration and wonders of the cave should read The Jewel Cave Adventure: Fifty Miles of Discovery Under South Dakota *(Cave Books), by Herb and Jan Conn."*

Read Logan bread's lore on page 228.

Kathee Forman

Peach Fluff Cake

1 egg	¼ teaspoon salt
¾ cup sugar	2 to 3 fresh peaches, sliced
¼ cup milk	(or frozen, thawed
3 tablespoons vegetable oil	peach slices)
¼ teaspoon vanilla	¼ cup sugar
¼ teaspoon lemon extract	¼ teaspoon cinnamon
1 cup flour, sifted	
1½ teaspoons baking	
powder	

In a large bowl, beat egg with electric beater on high for 3 to 4 minutes. With beater still running, gradually add ½ cup sugar. Beat until light. Set aside. In a small bowl, mix together milk, oil, vanilla, and lemon extract. Set aside. In a medium bowl, stir together flour, baking powder, and salt. Stir flour mixture and milk mixture alternately in several parts into the egg mixture. Mix well with each addition. Pour into greased, floured, 8-inch round cake pan. Arrange peach slices on top. Mix together ¼ cup sugar and cinnamon, and sprinkle over peaches. Bake at 350°F for 40 minutes. Cool completely. Slice and wrap individual slices in plastic wrap. Eat as a snack on the trail, or enjoy as dessert after dinner.

• • • • • • • • • •

Kathee Forman grew up enjoying the outdoors. She had to—her dad is David Mahre, a mountain guide and ski adventurer. The entire family has always been involved in various outdoor activities. Kathee started hiking and skiing at a young age, and began climbing while in college. Later she took up snowshoeing. Kathee and her husband, Russ, live in Naches, Washington. She thinks that nothing in life could be better than living in the beautiful Cascades, and it gets better each year.

"In hindsight, I had no idea that a family springtime trip to Mount Stuart, when I was twelve years old, would one day have so much meaning to me. Being on Long's Pass, at the top of the ridge, with its cornices and steep face below, was something I had never experienced before. Not only was it almost overwhelming, but I was also scared to death. Now, such sights are part of my life. I wish I had known back then that one day I would come to really appreciate the beauty of raw nature."

See Kathee's recipe for Blueberry Buckle, page 62. Her dad, David Mahre, has a recipe for High-Energy Fruit Bars on page 54.

Ruth Ittner

Apricot Nut Loaf

1 cup finely chopped dried apricots	1 teaspoon salt
1 cup warm water	¼ cup safflower oil
2 cups flour	1 egg, beaten
¼ cup dry milk	¼ cup orange juice
2 teaspoons baking powder	1 cup walnuts, chopped

Soak the apricots in warm water for 15 minutes. Drain, saving ¼ cup of the liquid. In a large bowl, combine flours, dry milk, baking powder, and salt. In another bowl, combine oil, egg, reserved apricot liquid, and orange juice. Add this mixture to the flour mixture, then fold in the drained apricots and the walnuts. Stir just enough to moisten the dry ingredients. Spread in a greased and floured 9 x 5-inch loaf pan. Bake at 350°F for about 55 minutes, or until a toothpick inserted in the center comes out clean. Cool in the pan for 10 minutes, then remove and finish cooling it on a wire rack. Store in the refrigerator.

● ● ● ● ● ● ● ● ● ●

Ruth Ittner of Seattle, Washington, became a fifty-year member of The Mountaineers in 2004, where she has served on internal committees as well as agency advisory committees. In the early 1970s, Ruth worked as a research consultant with the Institute of Governmental Research and its successor, the Institute for Public Policy and Management at the University of Washington. After attending the first National Trails Symposium around this time, Ruth felt a calling to focus on trails. Now at age 85, she has wonderful memories of outdoor activities, including climbing, hiking, cross-country skiing, snowshoeing, and sailing. She finds that her love of the outdoors, healthy way of life, creativity, and memories of the beauty and silence found in wilderness bring healing. To keep these recreational opportunities open for future generations, The Mountaineers are partners with land management agencies.

"Like all outdoor people, I appreciate suitable trail food and consider this bread a real delicacy. I often use it for sandwiches, and it makes excellent snacks.

"One of my favorite dehydrated dinners is one that I prepare myself at home before outings. It includes home-dried cooked hamburger, zucchini, tomatoes, and onions. Prepare it in whatever proportions you prefer, and serve it with grated Parmesan cheese."

Kathee Forman

Blueberry Buckle

1¼ cups sugar
½ cup shortening
1 egg
2 cups flour, sifted
2 teaspoons baking powder
¼ teaspoon salt
½ cup milk
2 cups frozen blueberries (do not thaw)
⅓ cup flour, unsifted
½ teaspoon cinnamon
¼ cup butter or margarine, softened

In a large bowl, cream ¾ cup sugar and shortening. Add egg and beat until mixture is fluffy. In a medium bowl, mix sifted flour, baking powder, and salt. Add flour mixture to egg mixture, alternating with milk. Mix well with each addition. Fold in frozen blueberries. The batter will be thick. Spread in a greased, floured, 9-inch square cake pan. In a small bowl, prepare topping by combining ½ cup sugar, ⅓ cup unsifted flour, and cinnamon. Cut butter into dry ingredients until mixture resembles soft crumbs. Sprinkle over batter. Bake at 400°F for 40 to 45 minutes, or until topping is golden brown. Cool completely. Cut into squares. Wrap individual squares in plastic wrap.

* * * * * * * * * *

"Eat this delicious coffee cake as a snack on the trail, or serve for dessert after dinner. Or leave the cake waiting for you in the car when you return to the trailhead after a day hike."

See Kathee's recipe for Peach Fluff Cake, page 60. Her biography appears on the same page.

Darryl Lloyd

Mount Adams Logan Bread

2 cups water
7 cups whole wheat flour (2 pounds)
1⅔ cups brown sugar (¾ pound)
2½ cups dry milk (6 ounces)
1 tablespoon baking powder
1 tablespoon salt
1 cup honey
½ cup molasses
⅝ cup vegetable oil
¾ cup wheat germ

Mix all ingredients well. Turn into a greased 10 x 14-inch roasting pan (or equivalent). Bake at 300°F for a little over an hour (usually 1 hour and 10 minutes). When done, cut the loaf into 20 squares. Air dry the squares for about 20 minutes, or until they are semidry. Wrap each square in plastic wrap, and then put them into resealable plastic bags. This recipe yields approximately 5 pounds, which is about right for 4 people on a 5-day trip, allowing a 4-ounce square per person per day. The bread is palatable, moist, quite sweet, and remains fresh for 2 weeks or more even in hot weather. It does not fall apart under rough handling.

· · · · · · · · · ·

Darryl Lloyd of Hood River, Oregon, works full-time as a freelance photographer. The Wilderness Institute on Mount Adams set up by Darryl and his twin brother, Darvel, ended with the eruption of Mount St. Helens in 1980. Darryl resumed a seafaring career, and worked worldwide as a ship captain. He gave that up in 1990 to help Darvel run the family's Flying L Ranch Inn (which was sold in 1997). Darryl's photography appears in regional and national publications, and is regularly exhibited in Columbia Gorge galleries. To learn more about Darryl's work, visit *www.longshadowphoto.com.*

"As my twin brother, Darvel, said when he was codirector of our business some years ago, we have to be careful with the menus on our outings for several reasons. We are catering to people from throughout North America with a great variety of tastes. Food must be appetizing and as varied as possible. Also, we are cooking over stoves at timberline and above, so we must make meals simple to cook. Food must be nutritious, with about 4,000 calories per person per day, and heavy in carbohydrates. It must also be lightweight. The total dry

weight of our meals runs a little more than 1¾ pounds per person per day (7 ounces for breakfast, 13 to 14 ounces for lunch, and 8 ounces for dinner).

"Breakfasts are usually a hot beverage and a hearty cereal with fruit. Lunches are the heavy items, like Logan Bread, cheese, and nuts, which are nibbled on throughout the day. Dinners consist of a hot drink, soup mix, a freeze-dried main course (usually improved by adding vegetables, margarine, and spices), and an instant pudding. Before the trip, all breakfasts and dinners are bagged and labeled, so there is a minimum of confusion in camp and exactly the right amount of food for the entire outing."

Read Logan bread's lore on page 228.

Sam Curtis

Whole Wheat Backpacking Bread

1 tablespoon dry yeast
1 tablespoon brown sugar
¼ cup lukewarm water
5 cups whole wheat flour
½ cup dry milk
2 cups warm water

1 tablespoon salt
3 tablespoons butter,
   margarine, oil, or
   melted bacon fat
6 tablespoons honey

Dissolve yeast and brown sugar in ¼ cup lukewarm water. Mix together the flour and dry milk. Mix the 2 cups of water, salt, shortening, and honey. Combine the yeast with the flour mixture. Add the liquid ingredients, and stir well. Put the dough into 2 greased 8½ x 4½ x 2½-inch loaf pans. Let rise in a warm place for 1 hour. Bake at 400°F for about 45 minutes.

· · · · · · · · · · ·

Sam Curtis of Bozeman, Montana, is editor of *Montana Wildlife Journal*. He has hiked extensively in the United States, Canada, and Europe, and has led mountain, desert, and cold-weather trips throughout the West. Sam is author of *Harsh Weather Camping* (Menasha Ridge Press). He has been a contributing editor for *Adventure Travel, Backpacking Journal*, and *Camping Journal*, and contributes to such magazines as *Audubon, Backpacker*, and *E: The Environmental Magazine*.

"One of the most leisurely camp meals I've ever had was in a snow cave at 10,500 feet on the side of Mount Cowan in the Montana Rockies. We had spent a lot of time slogging along on skis and shoveling snow before we could crawl into our makeshift home. Darkness slammed down by 5 P.M., leaving three or four hours before we would feel ready for the sack. Our multicourse meal, however, depended on melted snow as a basic ingredient, so we spent a good deal of that time sitting around the sputtering stove, mulling over the day's progress, and speculating on the possibility of reaching the summit the next morning.

"Cups of pea soup slowly gave way to 'cheese mac,' which faded into rehydrated meat bars, which lingered into copious cups of extra-thick hot chocolate. It was a repast of three hours in the cooking and eating—a very civilized meal in companionable surroundings, and an excellent way to pass the dark evening.

"We didn't make it to the summit of Mount Cowan the next day. A foot of new snow sealed over the snow cave during the night. This persuaded us not to dig out till oxygen seemed in short supply. We managed to ski down the glacial cirque without starting an avalanche and were thankful for that."

Bill Kemsley

Horn Creek Bannocks

2 cups biscuit mix
⅔ cup water (approximate)
Margarine to grease frying pan
Jam, etc., to taste

Combine biscuit mix and enough water to make a stiff dough. Pat a chunk of the dough into an inch-thick cake, as large as can fit into your frying pan, and fry it very slowly in margarine, turning often. It takes a long time, but it is a great dish if you have the time and a lot to talk about. Serves 2 to 4. Cook up a batch of these to enjoy as a snack.

● ● ● ● ● ● ● ● ● ●

Bill Kemsley, founder and former editor of *Backpacker* magazine, continues to write books on backpacking at his cabin in the woods in northern New Mexico. He also teaches classes in outdoor photography.

"I used to sail and in the mid-1950s was a mountain climber. I practiced in the Shawangunks in southeastern New York, where I put up a couple of new routes. I also climbed in other eastern rock climbing areas. I have made ascents in the Bugaboos of British Columbia, and in the Cascades, Tetons, and Rockies. In fact, I believe I have been on mountaineering or backpacking trips in every major mountain range in the continental United States. My wife, Marcella, and my six children found that backpacking was a great family activity.

"We have backpacked in Great Britain, the Virgin Islands, some of the choicest hiking areas of the United States, and several provinces in Canada. Besides where we currently live, the area we like best is the Catskill Mountains in southeastern New York west of the Hudson River.

"An exciting family trip was a seven-day backpack into the Grand Canyon. At that time our oldest child was thirteen, our youngest (carried by my wife) was nine months, and we had three toddlers. I don't believe in trying to get children to set records in hiking; but we couldn't help being proud of our youngsters, who hiked eleven miles in one day and made a vertical elevation gain of 4,000 feet in about four and a half hours. On that trip, we spent an entire afternoon cooking and eating bannocks with strawberry jam and Danish salami. We used up an entire box of biscuit mix and had an enormously good time."

Read bannock's lore on page 226.

Peter Simer

Cornmeal Flat Bread

½ cup flour
½ cup cornmeal
½ cup water
Pinch salt
Margarine
Cheese, thinly sliced
Bacon bits, or sliced sausage

Combine flour, cornmeal, and water. Form into flat patties. Fry in a frying pan lightly greased with margarine. When bottoms of patties are golden brown, turn them over. Place cheese and meat on top of patties, cover frying pan, and continue to cook until bottoms are nicely browned and the cheese is melted. (If cooking can be done over a campfire, fry patties till brown on both sides; place cheese and meat on top; melt cheese by placing hot coals on the frying pan lid for 5 to 10 minutes.) Serves 1 or 2.

• • • • • • • • • •

Peter Simer of Waterloo, Iowa, has extensive outdoor experience. He has spent long periods in the Rockies and Cascades as well as considerable time in Alaska, Baja California, Kenya, and the French Alps. He was the executive director of the National Outdoor Leadership School (NOLS) from 1975 to 1983. His students and staff adapted the Cornmeal Flat Bread and Syrian Bread recipes for backpacking.

"NOLS was founded in 1965 to train interested persons in the skills and judgment necessary for leadership in outdoor activities. The courses emphasize both the enjoyment and the conservation of the wild outdoors. With courses lasting from 14 to 114 days, there is a demand for good food made from grocery store ingredients.

"Another good recipe for outdoor baking—when you have time for it—is Syrian Bread. This version was created on Mount McKinley to supplement the repetitious diet on a six-week expedition. You need three ¼-ounce envelopes of dry yeast, ¼ cup warm water, a little sugar, and 1 cup each white and whole wheat flour (plus some extra flour). To water that is warm to the touch (not hot), add sugar and yeast. Let it work 5 to 10 minutes. Stir in flour. Knead, adding more flour as necessary, until the ball of dough is smooth. Put dough in a billycan and cover with a damp cloth. Let rise about an hour in a warm

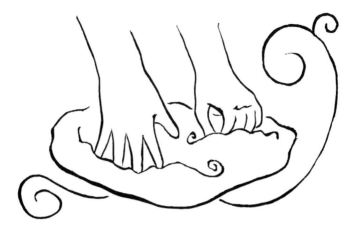

place. Punch down the dough. Pinch off lumps an inch in diameter. Flatten the lumps between the palms of your hands, and let rise 15 minutes. Place the lumps of dough one by one on a pan lid, or other flat surface, covered with a floured plastic sack. Using a clean water bottle for a rolling pin, roll each lump out to ⅛-inch thickness. Cook each piece separately in a covered frying pan, with no grease. When the loaf puffs up in the middle, flip it over and cook on the other side till golden brown. Slice the finished loaf in half—there should be a pocket in each half. Serve with butter, or with a spicy lentil filling."

R. J. Secor

Character-Assessment Gorp

1 pound peanuts
1 pound raisins
1 pound M&Ms

Mix the ingredients in a large paper shopping bag. Pour into a resealable plastic bag. Place in another plastic bag. Yields 3 pounds.

● ● ● ● ● ● ● ● ● ●

"I typically eat one pound of gorp in a week. If someone shares this gorp with you, don't be the kind of person who picks all of the M&Ms out of the mix, leaving only peanuts and raisins!"

See R.J.'s recipe for Vision Quest Refried Beans & Rice, page 104, and Coffee Can Cheesecake, page 144. His biography appears on page 104.

Read gorp's lore on page 226.

Dee Molenaar

Papaya-Licorice Gorp

Peanuts
Raisins
Dried papaya
Dried pineapple
Dried pears
Licorice-flavored candies or gumdrops
M & Ms

Mix ingredients in amounts needed and in any proportions, to taste. Dried papaya and pineapple can be found in the gourmet sections of health food stores or in the bulk food sections of grocery stores; they give a little different flavor to trail food.

• • • • • • • • • •

Dee Molenaar of Burley, Washington, is a veteran climber of varied and extensive experience. He was a guide on Mount Rainier in the early 1940s and a national park ranger between 1948 and 1952. In 1946 he was with an expedition that was the second to climb 18,008-foot Mount St. Elias on the Alaska-Canada border. At least nine previous attempts had been made on St. Elias; the Duke of Abruzzi led the only successful one, fifty years before. In addition to numerous climbs of Mount Rainier, on at least twelve different routes, he was a member of the historic 1953 American attempt on K2. In 1965 Dee was with a party that accompanied Senator Robert F. Kennedy on the first ascent of Mount Kennedy in the Yukon Territory. In 1990 he made a map-preparation and geological reconnaissance of a route to Mount Everest. Dee is an Honorary Member of The Mountaineers and The American Alpine Clubs.

"A somewhat startling food incident, 'The Case of the Instant Flambeau Dinner,' occurred when Forrest Johnson and I were climbing Mount Adams. I made the mistake of carrying drinking water and gasoline in identical plastic bottles. You can imagine what followed. When preparing dinner, I realized what had happened when a flame flickered over the surface of the soup in a pot."

Read gorp's lore on page 226.

Richard J. Tucker

Olde English Plum Pudding

1-pound loaf white bread
Water to cover bread
1 pound seeded muscat raisins
1 pound seedless raisins
1 pound currants
⅛ pound candied citron, cut small
Grated rind and juice of 1 orange
Grated rind and juice of 1 lemon
½ cup sugar
½ pound white kidney suet, chopped fine or ground (get suet from butcher)
½ cup all-purpose flour
1 teaspoon cinnamon
½ teaspoon allspice
½ teaspoon salt
Eggs, 2 for each bowl used for steaming pudding
Baking powder, 2 teaspoons per bowl used for steaming pudding

Soak the loaf of bread in water overnight. Squeeze out excess water, and beat bread till light with electric mixer or mixing spoon. Combine the bread, fruits, sugar, suet, flour, spices, and salt. Grease eight to twelve 6-inch diameter bowls well, and fill each about ⅔ full of batter. To each bowl, add 2

eggs and 2 teaspoons baking powder, and mix thoroughly into batter in the bowl. Cover each bowl with cheesecloth tied tightly over the top with string. In a large kettle or kettles that can be tightly covered, set bowls of batter on a rack in boiling water that comes about halfway up the bowls. Cover the kettles and steam the puddings for 5 or 6 hours. Maintain the water level by carefully adding more boiling water as necessary.

The finished puddings can be cut up and eaten as snacks or desserts. The pudding tastes best reheated and is very good served with hard sauce (a blend of powdered sugar, butter, and a dash of salt, with a flavoring such as vanilla, rum, etc.). People have been known to carry in a little brandy, which can be poured over the pudding, lighted, and served flaming on a cold night.

● ● ● ● ● ● ● ● ● ●

Richard Tucker has been doing adventurous activities in the mountains since the late 1960s. While most of his climbing has been in New England, he has also visited many other places in the United States and Canada, as well as four other continents. In winter, Richard particularly likes cross-country skiing and snowshoeing in the White Mountains of New Hampshire. In summer when he is not climbing or hiking, he enjoys bicycling, sailing, and kayaking. He is currently president of an engineering consulting company based in Waltham, Massachusetts.

"I have been climbing and backpacking since the late 1960s, mostly in New England in all seasons. I have also taken trips in the Colorado Rockies, the Tetons and Wind Rivers in Wyoming, the Cascades of Washington, Glacier National Park in Montana, the San Francisco Peaks and Grand Canyon areas of Arizona, the Canadian Rockies, the Alps, and the Andes. I am a member of the National Ski Patrol and participate in kayaking, white-water canoeing, and long-distance ocean races. For lunches and snacks I like breads that are dense, moist, high in nutrition, and not easily crushed. The ultimate in calories and nutrition seems to be found in my great-grandmother's plum pudding recipe—it is very complicated, but I think worth the effort. If properly made, the pudding keeps indefinitely without refrigeration."

Steven Schneider and Anne Sequoia

Mountain Mandelbrodt

1 cup sugar
4 large eggs
²⁄₃ cup vegetable shortening
1¾ cups seedless raisins or currants
2 cups chopped walnuts
⅓ cup each orange and lemon juice
4½ cups unbleached presifted flour (don't resift)
4 teaspoons baking powder
¼ cup sugar
1 teaspoon cinnamon
¼ teaspoon vanilla
Pinch salt

Put sugar and 2 of the eggs into an electric blender. Blend at medium speed for 2 minutes till almost smooth. Add remaining eggs and shortening. Blend at high speed till smooth, 1½ to 2 minutes. Pour the batter into a large bowl. Add raisins and stir by hand till batter coats raisins. Add nuts and stir till coated. Add fruit juices and vanilla. Stir in 2 cups of the flour by hand. Add remaining flour, baking powder, and salt. Mix vigorously for 4 or 5 minutes till well blended. The dough will be thick and heavy, and requires a climber's muscles to mix. Refrigerate dough for 15 minutes.

With lightly floured hands, pinch pieces of dough about the size of small baked potatoes, form them into thick sausage shapes, and flatten slightly. Place on 2 greased cookie sheets, spacing the loaves well apart. Combine the ¼ cup sugar with cinnamon, and sprinkle generously over the flattened tops. Bake at 325°F until evenly browned; watch closely after the first 30 minutes. Mandelbrodt is ready to eat when cool, but should be aged for 2 or 3 days before being taken on a trip.

• • • • • • • • • •

Steven Schneider and his sister, Anne Sequoia, used to own a climbing school and guide service in New England. Steven has rock- and ice-climbed extensively in New England, the Dolomites of Italy, and the mountain cliffs near the Mediterranean in France. Anne has backpacked from Switzerland to northern Greece. Anne, a successful author, is currently writing a novel. She also collects vintage mountaineering books. Steven lives in Shelburne, Vermont, and is an independent sales rep for outdoor equipment, backpacking, mountaineering, and kayaking gear.

Steven also works with the Green Mountain Council of the Boy Scouts of America.

"Mandelbrodt is found in most Slavic countries, and probably in Austria and Germany. Some cooks use only raisins, some only nuts, and some add chocolate. Any way you make it, it's wonderful Big Wall food. A few winters ago a friend and I were climbing the 600-foot icicle on the Black Dike of Cannon Cliff and took a break to eat. At 20 degrees below, the mandelbrodt was frozen, but those wonderful icy chunks kept us going."

Joan Firey

Fruit-Nut Rolls

Dried fruits and nuts in equal amounts (good combinations include raisins/walnuts, dates/pecans, and apricots/almonds)

Grind the fruit and nuts in a meat grinder. Mix well. Roll into balls 1 inch to 1½ inches in diameter. Wrap each ball in foil.

•   •   •   •   •   •   •   •   •   •

The late Joan Firey of Seattle, Washington, was involved in alpine and expedition climbing from 1948 until shortly before her death in early 1980. She was a skilled artist and outdoor cook. Her favorite mountaineering area was the Picket Range in the North Cascades, where she made the first winter ascent of Mount Terror in 1977. Joan also climbed in California, Alaska, Mexico, and Peru. In 1978 she was a member of the American Women's Himalayan Expedition that put two women and two Sherpas on the summit of 26,545-foot Annapurna I.

Joan was in charge of the high-altitude menus for the Annapurna expedition. She also wrote the section on alpine cuisine for the second and third editions of *Mountaineering: The Freedom of the Hills* (The Mountaineers Books).

All my artwork is outdoor related, whether of small details of flowers and trees, or rocks, or mountain panoramas. I am primarily a watercolorist, though I also work in acrylics and oils and do some serigraphs.

"When planning meals for backpacking and climbing, I feel that lunch munching is important, and so is choosing lunch foods to suit a variety of conditions (length of day, type of activity, weather, etc.). Sandwiches are fine. Fresh fruits and vegetables are a nice addition in summer. Richer, heavier foods are needed in winter. I always weigh my lunch foods, especially for trips longer than a weekend—lunch food can easily equal or surpass the weight of dehydrated breakfasts and dinners. Ten ounces of carefully planned lunch food per day is adequate to generous, though on long trips I allow more to accommodate increased appetites. My specialty for extended trips or bivouac climbs is the following mixture, which looks terrible but is a real sustainer. Mix thoroughly a 4½-ounce meat bar, 4½ ounces peanut butter, and 4 ounces of raisins ground in a meat grinder. Form into 3 or 4 portions and wrap in foil."

John Fischer

Lead Bread

2 cups water
4 cups flour (a mixture of rye, whole wheat, etc., to taste)
½ to 1 teaspoon salt
2 cups dried fruit and nuts (dates, figs, pitted prunes, apples, broken cashews, etc., in proportions to taste)

Mix all ingredients. Spread dough about 2 inches thick in a lightly oiled loaf pan, or form into a flat lump. Bake at 200°F for about 3 hours, with oven door slightly ajar. The bread is done when the moisture is gone and the loaf sounds hollow when you thump it. Amounts given in the recipe can be varied to make more or less, depending on need.

● ● ● ● ● ● ● ● ● ●

John Fischer of Half Moon Bay, California, has made ascents in mountain ranges throughout the western United States and Canada, climbed the Mexican volcanoes, been on expeditions to Mount McKinley and Mount Logan, and made Big Wall climbs in Yosemite and in the Andes. After thirty-one years as a mountain guide, he retired and now makes solo climbs and surfs. His other interests include photography and taking to the road on his motorcycle.

"We ate Lead Bread during our twenty-one-day trip up 22,834-foot Aconcagua in Argentina. But it had taken a whole day to find a baker who would make it in expedition quantity. This brick-like loaf is a mutation of the famed Logan Bread. Due to its consistency and simple ingredients, it will keep indefinitely and survive the most rigorous transport (even airdrops) as long as it remains dry. You can really depend on its not going bad or turning to crumbs. Many a time have my mates and I divvied up the day's portion with an ice ax. If you manage to slice it thin enough, this bread tastes almost like whole grain rye crackers, and it's good served with jam and butter. It can be moistened by immersion in soup or other liquids. Once at Kluane Lake, we let it sit out in the rain to reduce it to an edible sogginess."

Morris Jenkins

Fruit-Nut Pemmican

2 cups mixed nuts
1½ cups raisins
8 ounces dried dates
8 ounces dried beef or jerky
Honey to make stiff dough
Salt, to taste

Grind up nuts, raisins, dates, and meat. Mix thoroughly in a large bowl. Stir in enough honey to give the mixture the consistency of stiff dough. Add salt if needed (some kinds of dried beef or jerky contain enough salt). Pack in double resealable plastic bags, and store in a durable paper bag or a covered ice cream container for protection in your pack. A tablespoon of this pemmican between 2 slices of bread makes a satisfying meal.

● ● ● ● ● ● ● ● ●

Morris Jenkins of Cle Elum, Washington, was a professional forester for over forty years and a backpacker longer than that.

"My wife, Sue, and I spent our honeymoon in 1932 in the Cascades north of Cle Elum. One day we started uptrail with no packs and only a sandwich between us. We got to a rugged rock spire between Hyas and Deep Lakes, now called Cathedral Rock. Then it was known as Jimmy's Jumpoff—after Jimmy Grieve, an early-day gold miner, who had once backpacked a woodstove from Fish Lake to his cabin behind the spire.

"Nobody in our area had any climbing equipment in the early 1930s. We just decided to climb the 6724-foot spire. It was difficult going in places. About 150 feet from the top, there was a chockstone in a chimney. I got past the obstacle, Sue came up, and in a short time we scrambled to the top. There was a register there, and as far as we know Sue was the first woman to make the climb.

"By then it was quite late. Down near Peggy's Pond we could see Jimmy's old cabin. We reached the cabin just before dark, with hopes of finding food. There was some flour in a can, but it was so ancient it had turned yellow; the pancakes I made were inedible. Grouse season was open, but I had no gun. I managed to hit a fool hen with a rock, and then cut it up to broil on sticks over the campfire. Sue claims it was cooked three ways—burned, raw, and well done; she couldn't force it down.

"After spending the night curled up on an old mattress in the cabin, I managed to eat a little more fool hen—but not so Sue. We then climbed 7986-foot, glacier-covered Mount Daniel. We came down the cliffs above Hyas Lake, only to find there was no shoreline. Luckily I spotted a raft nearby, so I poled us across to the Fish Lake Trail. That night we spent in a ranger's cabin where I had left ample food when on a Forest Service job. But Sue was too tired to eat. It was quite an experience to do all that on one sandwich and a couples of bites of fool hen."

Read pemmican's lore on page 228.

Savory Salads

*Y*ou might not crave salads much at home, but for some reason, after a few days on the trail, you might be surprised that you'd really like one. Don't worry, included here are a few tried-and-true zesty salads.

Most are easy to assemble at home and require rehydration. At breakfast, add water to the salads, and they'll be rehydrated by break time.

Salads provide a nice side dish to the dinners found in the next chapter, "Celebrate the Day Dinners," beginning on page 87. Also, a salad and a hunk of hearty bread combine to make a great lunch!

Now . . . as mom used to say, "Eat your greens!"

June Fleming

Trail-Happy Salad

2 cups dried shredded cabbage
1 cup dried shredded carrots
½ cup dried pineapple bits or raisins (or combine both)
1 tablespoon sugar
1 tablespoon vinegar
1 tablespoon vegetable oil
Salt, to taste

At home, combine cabbage and carrots. Place in a resealable plastic bag. Pack pineapple and/or raisins in a separate plastic bag. In a small leak-proof plastic bottle, combine sugar, vinegar, oil, and salt. At camp, before starting to cook dinner, add cold water to cover the dry mix in the plastic bag. Seal bag, then "knead" gently to moisten dried vegetables. Let stand about 30 minutes. Drain off excess liquid (into a soup or stew pot, if you've got one going). Shake dressing, and pour into bag. Seal bag and mix well. Serves 6.

• • • • • • • • • •

"I love to eat well on outdoor adventures, but with a minimum of fuss and time in the camp kitchen. Getting a food dehydrator years ago was the move that led to a wealth of varied meals and snacks, a lot of fun, and money saved. Make your own strawberry-rhubarb leather, almost-instant applesauce, spaghetti sauce, or other foods. Why buy these things when you can easily dry them at home? We dry bargain-priced bananas all year round, to be used for our own trips, as gifts and trades, and as at-home snacks. Purchased dehydrated bananas taste like honey-coated styrofoam compared to these delicious slices."

See June's recipes for Protein Power Muffins, page 34, S'Mores Bars, page 150, and Trail Coffees, page 160. Her biography appears on page 34.

Chester T. Rice

Pennsylvania Dutch Salad

> 2 ounces dried vegetable mix
> ¼ bacon bar, or bacon bits (¾ ounces)
> ¼ cup grated Swiss cheese
> ½ cup garlic-flavored croutons
> ⅛ to ¼ cup ranch-style salad dressing

Rehydrate vegetable mix by covering with cold water and soaking for 15 to 20 minutes. Drain, then add remaining ingredients. Serves 2.

• • • • • • • • • •

Chester T. (Chet) Rice lives in Kentfield, California, near San Francisco. He started backpacking in the mid-1930s with a packbasket in the Adirondacks. Now retired, Chester owned Smilie Company, a San Francisco camping outfitter. He can often be found with his family, driving his 1978 VW camper to their cabin near the Desolation Wilderness trailhead, in the Lake Tahoe area. Chester considers himself particularly fortunate to have had many camping experiences, and encourages everyone to go out and explore, have fun, and eat well in the backcountry.

"When planning food for an outing, first write down the entire menu for the trip, and assemble a shopping list from that. Dehydrated and freeze-dried foods can be supplemented with a careful selection of quick-cooking items from your local grocery store. Try to minimize weight and bulk, and to maximize ease of preparation and appetite appeal.

"Figure on about 2 pounds of lightweight dehydrated and freeze-dried food per person per day. The need varies with the individual, but a typical adult diet runs about 3500 calories per day for backpacking. Most dehydrated foods provide around 100 calories per ounce; powdered eggs and margarine provide about 200 calories per ounce.

"Remember that cooking time at 8000 feet elevation is about double that at sea level. A 1-pot meal for 2 persons requires a 1- to 1½-quart cooking pot, and for 4 persons a 2-quart pot. A lightweight frying pan is handy, and for some menus necessary. Cook over a one-burner stove in most places.

"To make a savory omelet, stir ⅓ cup cold water gradually into 2 ounces (4 tablespoons) dried egg. Add 1 teaspoon dried red or green pepper, 2 teaspoons dry onion, a crushed chicken bouillon cube, and 1 or 2 pinches garlic powder. Soak for 5 to 10 minutes. Fry in 1 tablespoon margarine or olive oil."

Glenn Porzak

Hindu Kush Salad

Bacon (or artificial bacon bits)
Onion (fresh, or reconstituted dry)
Swiss cheese
Vegetable or melted bacon fat
Vinegar

Fry bacon, drain off grease, and crumble. Rehydrate dry onion, or chop fresh onion very fine. Dice cheese into very small pieces. Combine oil (or melted bacon fat) and vinegar in desired proportions for dressing. Toss dressing with other mixture.

● ● ● ● ● ● ● ● ● ●

Glenn Porzak is an attorney from Boulder, Colorado, who is a past president of both the American Alpine Club and the Colorado Mountain Club. He has personally summitted three 8000-meter peaks (Shisha Pangma in 1983; Makalu in 1987; and Mount Everest in 1990) and led the first American ascent of Lhotse in 1990. He has climbed the Seven Summits and was the first person to climb the 100 highest peaks in Rocky Mountain National Park. Worldwide, he has made more than 1200 separate ascents of different peaks on all seven continents.

"Most of my climbing has been done in the Colorado Rockies, where I have made more than 400 ascents, including the Diamond on Longs Peak and several first ascents. In 1974 I became the first person to have climbed all ninety-eight named peaks over 11,000 feet in Rocky Mountain National Park. I have also climbed extensively in the Swiss and French Alps, and in Alaska.

"I have been on overseas expeditions to Noshaq (24,580 feet elevation) and Korpusht-e-Yakhi (18,688 feet) in the Hindu Kush Range of Afghanistan; to Aconcagua (22,834 feet) in Argentina; and Kilimanjaro and Kenya in Africa. I was leader of the 1978 Colorado Himalayan Expedition that attempted 26,760-foot Manaslu in the Gorkha Himalaya of central Nepal, only a few miles from the Tibetan-Chinese frontier.

"The one unsatisfied craving often mentioned by climbers on expeditions or other extended mountain trips is salad. It was while I was climbing in the Hindu Kush in 1975 that I came across an Austrian expedition that had solved the problem under conditions where fresh salad greens simply were unavailable. Their Hindu Kush Salad gave the impression of eating a real salad, and it was delicious."

Jay Zane Walley

Backpack-Gardener's Salad

1 cup mixed sprouts
Any wild food available, such as grains, onion, dock root,
**   watercress, etc.**
Peanuts (unsprouted)
Sunflower seeds (unsprouted)
Vegetable oil
Vinegar
Salt and pepper

Mix sprouts with any wild foods that are appropriate and available.
Sprinkle with peanuts and sunflower seeds. Make a dressing by combining oil, vinegar, and seasonings; pour over salad. Serves 2.

• • • • • • • • • •

Jay Zane Walley is a backpacker, climber, and cross-country skier who
particularly enjoys the High Sierra and the desert mountains of Nevada.

*"One of my greatest passions is Nevada's desert ranges. When you penetrate
these barren-looking regions by foot or on skis, you find oases with cottonwood
trees, watercress—sometimes even wild mustangs. Above 7000 feet, you may
have superb trout fishing.*

*"After a week on the trail, you long for the high delight of a fresh salad. With
great ease and little expense, you can become a backpack-gardener, growing
vegetables right in your pack. All you need is small heavy-duty garbage bags
and a supply of untreated seeds available in any grocery or health food store.
Mung, adzuki, or other beans; alfalfa seeds; hulled pumpkin or sunflower seeds;
peas; wheat; and hulled peanuts are all excellent, as they are high in protein
and vitamins.*

*"To start sprouts at home, put ¼ to 1 cup seeds into a wide-mouthed jar. Cover
seeds with lukewarm water and soak overnight. Drain. Keep jar on its side in
a dark place, or cover with a towel or paper bag. Rinse sprouts 2 to 4 times
daily with lukewarm water—this keeps them damp and improves flavor. After
each rinsing, drain (easy if you cover the jar mouth with cheesecloth or piece of
nylon stocking). Before the backpack, transfer sprouts to resealable plastic bags
(double, to prevent leaks). Keep on top of your pack so they won't be crushed
and are accessible for rinsing (use tepid canteen water, as cold water retards
growth). While hiking, start new sprouts in plastic bags as you go along. You*

eat the sprouts, seeds and all. When sprouts have reached edible size, keep them cool if possible and they will stay fresh for about a week.

"Another good way to prepare sprouts in camp is to use your cooking pot as a 'walking wok.' Heat oil in a pot. Drop in ½ cup of rehydrated freeze-dried vegetables. Stir-fry for 2 or 3 minutes. Add a package of reconstituted dehydrated eggs, and scramble till sticky. Add 1 cup sprouts (any type), and cook till done. Season with soy sauce to taste, or with salt and pepper."

Celebrate the Day: Dinners

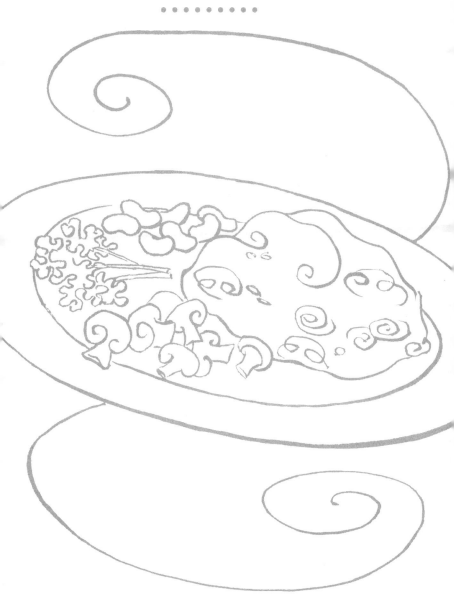

*A*t the end of the day, dinner is a welcome reward. And "dinner will be ready in 20 minutes" are words everyone likes to hear. Even if you're not a great cook, the meals you'll find in this chapter are easy to fix. You can keep it simple with one-pot dinners and tempting stews, creative noodle dishes, and gourmet ethnic-inspired dishes. Seasoned outdoorspeople have put these meals to the test and shared their tips. Now you can enjoy them too.

Many of the dishes can be assembled at home, stored in resealable plastic bags, and stowed in your pack. At camp, they are a snap to pull together. Some are as simple as a "doctored-up" pre-packaged dinner, while others are favorite family recipes that have been adapted for camp cooking.

If you're the designated cook, you could even whip up a batch of appetizers—there are a couple to choose from—to stave off the hungry hordes until dinner is ready. Your dinner companions will be impressed.

Try them all, then experiment with your favorite ingredients to create your own delicious dinners. You might just discover that you can expand your list of favorite trail recipes.

Don't forget that salads make great side dishes. The previous chapter, "Savory Salads," beginning on page 79, offers a few that will round out your dinners.

Now grab a pot and stirring implement and get to it. In no time, you'll be chowing down and lickin' your lips. Ummm, good!

Dennis Lewon

Canyon Crostinis

1 cup dried porcini mushrooms, sliced
1 cup sun-dried tomatoes, sliced
¼ cup olive oil
3 cloves garlic, chopped
½ cup pine nuts
½ cup fresh basil
Salt and pepper, to taste
7.5-ounce package crostinis (small toasts)

Soak the mushrooms and tomatoes in hot water for 5 minutes. Remove from water. Heat olive oil in a pan and sauté the mushrooms and tomatoes, adding garlic and pine nuts. Stir in salt, pepper, and basil just before removing mixture from heat. Serve as dip with crostinis. This tasty appetizer is a quick, lightweight, and easy way to add flair to any meal. Serves 4.

● ● ● ● ● ● ● ● ● ●

See Dennis's recipe for Trail Tiramisu, page 143. His biography appears on the same page.

Ted Millan

Makemwait Mushrooms

1½ cup dried, sliced portobello mushrooms (or white
    mass-grown variety)
1 to 2 tablespoons olive oil
½ cup water
Lemon pepper, to taste

Rehydrate mushrooms in a resealable plastic bag (using equal parts mushrooms and water), or place mushrooms in a frying pan and barely cover with water. When rehydrated, drain excess water. Stir and slowly cook mushrooms until water is nearly gone. Add 1 tablespoon oil and continue stirring until mushrooms are thoroughly hot. Add more oil if necessary. Sprinkle lemon pepper over top. Serves 4, as an appetizer.

• • • • • • • • • •

Ted Millan of Seattle, Washington, is an attorney who enjoys hiking, backpacking, cross-country skiing, snow caving, and snow camping. He was active in Scouts for many years, and still goes on an occasional Scout outing. He began dehydrating food at home ten years ago, seeking to make good food that weighed little and was easy to prepare. He won the REI Camp Stove Cook Off in 2001.

"Our Scout troop's annual fifty-mile hike is popular and gives me a chance to experiment and learn. During one week in Idaho a few years ago, the boys tried to hurry me and get me to cut corners when they sensed the food was almost ready. When cooking with dehydrated food you must let everything fully rehydrate, which is difficult when the boys gather around with plates and forks in hand. The results were some undercooked meals. I came up with this simple appetizer to keep the boys occupied while I finish cooking. It's a quick and easy morale builder, and weighs almost nothing."

See Ted's recipe for Angry Moose Scrambled Eggs, page 20 and Old Goats' One-Pot Ginger Cashew Chicken Fried Rice, page 102. "Ted Millan's Trail Food–Drying Basics" can be found on page 221.

Dorcas Miller

Cashew-Ginger Chicken and Rice

½ cup cashews, toasted and cooled
1 cup instant brown rice, uncooked
⅔ cups freeze-dried corn or ½ cup dried veggie of choice
½ cup dry shiitake mushrooms, sliced thin
¼ cup onion flakes
1 10-ounce can chicken, mixed white and dark meat
1 packet (1 ounce) Thai coconut ginger soup mix paste

At home, place cashews in a resealable plastic bag. Combine rice, dried corn or veggie, mushrooms, and onion flakes and place in another resealable plastic bag. At camp, place the dry mix, chicken, and soup mix in a pot and cover with water; mix well. Bring to a boil and simmer 5 minutes (adding more water as needed) or until done. Serve sprinkled with cashews. Serves 2.

Variations: Substitute almonds for cashews, lemon-pepper seasoning for ginger, or savoy cabbage and carrots for corn. (To dry cabbage, slice ⅛ inch thick and sprinkle in a thin layer on nonstick cookie sheet. For carrots, shred and sprinkle on cookie sheet. Place cookie sheet in 130°F oven, leaving door open 1 or 2 inches. Dehydrate veggies until done, stirring occasionally. When cooled, cabbage should be leathery and carrots dry but pliable.)

• • • • • • • • • •

Dorcas Miller, of Chelsea, Maine, has worked as an Outward Bound instructor, teacher, river guide, environmental advocate, and editor. She's written twelve books on outdoor adventure and natural history topics, including *Backcountry Cooking* (The Mountaineers Books) and *More Backcountry Cooking* (The Mountaineers Books), and is coordinator of Maine's Becoming an Outdoors-Woman program.

"I've been cooking on the trail for more than thirty years, and this is my all-time favorite dinner. It's a snap to make, easy to clean up after, and it consistently gets rave reviews. If I'm base-camping near a bear locker, I add cold water to the dry ingredients in the morning, place the pot in the locker, and let dinner rehydrate while I'm off hiking or rock climbing. In the evening I add chicken and heat—an instant dinner. On canoeing trips, I combine hot water and all ingredients, stir well, cover, and let stand while I go for a refreshing swim. When I return, I reheat and serve—no slaving over a hot fire."

Kristin Hostetter

Rodeo Rice

1 cup instant brown rice
½ cup dried vegetables
1 vegetable-flavored bouillon cube
Water
Olive oil
¼ cup pine nuts (preferably toasted)
Dried herbs, to taste (oregano, basil, or tarragon)
Salt and pepper, to taste
Tortillas (optional; enough for up to 4 people)

Place rice, vegetables, bouillon, and water (enough to cover plus 1 inch) in a wide-mouth Nalgene bottle (1 quart). Stow in your pack. When you're ready to eat, pour the rehydrated mixture into a cookpot or bowl. Stir in oil, pine nuts, herbs, and salt and pepper. Fluff with fork. Great with tortillas. Serves 4.

● ● ● ● ● ● ● ● ●

"Throw these few ingredients into a bottle at breakfast and you'll be dining in style at lunch. I came up with this on a trip in Wyoming's Wind River Range when the peanut butter ran dry and we still had a few days to go. The recipe's name is a tribute to the cowboys of Wyoming."

See Kristin's s recipe for Cascade Morning Couscous, page 19, and Off-Piste Pesto Pasta, page 119. Her biography appears on page 19.

Jane Wentworth

Sweet & Spicy Moroccan Stew Over Couscous

1 tablespoon fresh onion, minced or 1 teaspoon dried onion flakes
1 garlic clove, minced, or ½ teaspoon dried garlic
½ teaspoon ground cumin
1 teaspoon fresh ginger, minced, or ¼ teaspoon powdered ginger
¼ teaspoon ground coriander
¼ teaspoon ground cinnamon
¼ teaspoon tomato powder
1½ to 1¾ cups water
¼ to 1 teaspoon salt, or to taste
¾ cup plain couscous (quick-cooking variety, such as Near East brand)
3 teaspoons olive oil or butter
1 medium fresh carrot, chopped (about 1 cup)
1 small fresh zucchini, chopped (about 1 cup)
1 to 2 plum tomatoes (optional)
½ cup water
¼ cup sun-dried tomatoes, chopped or torn
½ cup dried fruit (currants, raisins, and/or chopped apricots)
¼ cup kalamata olives, pitted and sliced
Salt and red pepper, to taste
¼ cup almonds (raw or roasted), chopped

At home, for the stew, mix together the onion, garlic, cumin, ginger, coriander, cinnamon, and tomato powder. Store in a resealable plastic bag.

At camp, in a small saucepan, bring 1 cup water, 2 teaspoons olive oil, and salt to boil. Add couscous. Remove from heat. Cover, and let stand 5 minutes. To keep couscous warm, cover pan with a wool hat or towel. For the stew, in a small saucepan, heat 1 teaspoon olive oil, then sauté the carrots, zucchini, and tomato for about 1 minute. Stir in the stew mix. Add ½ cup water, sun-dried tomato, fruit, and olives. Simmer for 5 minutes until the liquid reduces to a sauce and the vegetables are tender, adding more water if needed. Salt and pepper to taste. Serve over cooked couscous. Top with chopped raw or roasted almonds. Serves 2.

This meal uses only 1½ to 1¾ cups water and takes less than 10 minutes to cook. Fresh carrots, zucchini, and plum tomatoes travel fairly well

and add fresher flavors, although dehydrated vegetables can also be used. To rehydrate, you will need to add more water as they cook.

• • • • • • • • •

See Jane's recipe for Comfort Pudding, page 148. Her biography appears on the same page.

Laura Waterman

Celebration Couscous

2 to 3 cups water
¼ to ½ cup freeze-dried peas
½ to 1 cup couscous
1 6-ounce can tuna
¼ cup butter, or margarine
Cheddar cheese, cut into 1-inch cubes
Salt and pepper, to taste

Bring water to boil. Add freeze-dried peas and bring back to boil. Add couscous, then tuna and butter. Stir until water is absorbed. If too thick, add more water. Serve in bowls, then salt and pepper to taste. Add the cheese chunks and let them melt as you eat. Don't add the cheese to the pot since it will stick and make for a tough cleanup job. Serves 2.

• • • • • • • • • •

Laura Waterman and her late husband, Guy, climbed in Alaska, the Canadian Rockies, and Newfoundland but made the White Mountains of New Hampshire their primary year-round stomping ground. Guy climbed New Hampshire's forty-eight 4000-footers from all four compass points in winter. Laura was the first woman to make a winter ascent of the Balack Dike on Cannon Cliff, and to lead Pinnacle Gully in Huntington Ravine on Mount Washington. They were early authors of books on low-impact camping and hiking, and also wrote on the history of mountaineering in the Northeast. The couple devoted twenty years to developing trail techniques that could hold up to the increasing numbers of hikers frequenting the alpine areas of their home mountains. Since Guy's death in 2000, the Guy Waterman Alpine Stewardship Fund was established to strengthen the human stewardship of the summits, ridgelines, and alpine areas of the Northeast, *www.watermanfund.org.*

"Celebration Couscous was Guy's and my favorite dinner, hands down. We made it our final meal for just about every trip we ever took, so we must have eaten it hundreds of times. Its great advantage (other than taste) is that you can prepare it under conditions of extreme exhaustion. You just have to remember to spill the ingredients into the pot (in any order) and stay awake long enough for it to thicken (only a few minutes). Then you can eat it with your eyes closed, even asleep; Guy swore I did that one time (though I don't remember this). Celebration Couscous was our mountain "comfort food," and don't worry if you forget to cut up the cheese. If you're asleep you won't miss it."

Barbara Coon

Grand Canyon Chile Relleños

2 7-ounce cans green chiles, drained
½ cup grated Monterey Jack or cheddar cheese
2 eggs
4 teaspoons cornmeal
Salt, to taste
Water
Oil for frying

Stuff each chile with cheese. Separate eggs into two bowls. Stir cornmeal and salt into yolks, adding a bit of water to make batter. Whisk egg whites until stiff peaks form. Coat stuffed chilies with egg whites, then dip chilies in batter. Let excess drip off into batter bowl. Heat oil in skillet. Fry chilies until golden brown (about 3 to 5 minutes per side). Serves 3. (Yields approximately 10 chili relleños, depending on the number in each can.)

● ● ● ● ● ● ● ● ●

Barbara Coon of Northern Virginia says that, after six decades of life, she has learned that the best advice is, "Always do more challenging things than you think you can, with people whose skills challenge you, without being a drag on the group. Soon enough you'll be helping others improve. Try everything. Go outdoors wherever you are. Something interesting always happens and you'll be glad that you were there to experience it."

"I made these chile relleños at the bottom of the canyon after someone handed me a margarita to help assuage the somewhat fussy nature of the prep. But it was worth it! A word of advice—try to keep the hordes away until you've cooked enough for each person to have one chile!

"Another of my favorite trail meals, for a first or second night, is clams with pasta. Pack as much garlic and fresh cilantro as you like. Chop them on a backpacking cutting board. Lightly brown the garlic in olive oil (packed in a small plastic bottle, and a resealable plastic bag). Next add a 6-ounce can of chopped clams. Raise heat slightly and let liquid reduce to half. Add the cilantro. Pour the clams into your eating dish. Use the same pot to cook whole wheat spaghetti or other pasta. Drain and add pasta to the clams. Top with lots of fresh-shaved Parmesan cheese. The saw blade on a Swiss Army knife is great for shaving cheese.

"A fellow hiker once observed, 'I believe you like to cook real food because you're in a real place.' He was right . . . and I think he hoped that I would share my meal."

Lynn Buchanan

Rainier Spotted Dog

3 cups water
1 package instant mashed potatoes
Cheddar cheese, shaved
2½ to 5 ounces dried (chipped) beef
Butter, salt, and pepper

Heat water. Add potatoes according to package directions, in any amount necessary for preferred thickness. Add desired quantities of cheese, chipped beef, butter, and flavorings. Serves 2.

• • • • • • • • • •

Lynn Buchanan of Yakima, Washington, has made many climbs in the Cascades, including over twenty ascents of Mount Adams by various routes, one in winter. He was in the group led by the late Hal Foss that first completed a high-level encirclement of Mount Rainier at about the 9000- or 10,000-foot level. In 1995, his party's ascent of 18,000-foot Orizaba in Mexico was successful. In 1998 and 2000 he participated in unsuccessful expeditions to Aconcagua. In 2003, the National Mountain Rescue Association recognized Lynn for his fifty years of mountain rescue. He is a pilot with seven thousand hours of flight time.

"The one-day climb up Rainier in late July each year took six months of planning. Between 400 and 500 people would sign up for the ascent. Meetings and physical conditioning programs were held to prepare participants. Experienced climbers volunteered as leaders and arrived on the mountain days ahead to get everything ready. They marked the route (on the easy south side) with bamboo wands, set up radio communication and a first-aid station, and arranged for Mountain Rescue personnel to be on hand. I most enjoyed taking people up who really wanted to climb but had never had an opportunity. It was a relatively safe way to have a mountain adventure. Two hundred to three hundred would reach the summit after a 6000-foot gain in elevation. Participants either got so tired they never wanted to climb again, or else became climbers from then on.

"We had some humorous incidents. One fellow carried up a two-foot mirror to signal to his friends in Yakima. My younger brother had often heard our route referred to as so easy it was a 'grandmother's hike,' so he backpacked a rocking chair to the summit. He was among the first to arrive and rocked away in his chair as others finished the climb. We discouraged dogs after the time I returned to camp to find a dog wolfing down the steak I had been looking forward to all day."

Corinne Humphrey

Moroccan Keftas

1 pound ground meat
1 onion, chopped
2 mint leaves, chopped
2 tablespoons parsley, chopped
2 tablespoons cilantro, chopped
½ teaspoon ground cumin
½ teaspoon turmeric
1 teaspoon paprika
¼ teaspoon chili powder
Salt and pepper, to taste
Couscous or rice (optional)
Skewers

In a bowl, combine meat, onion, mint, parsley, cilantro, cumin, turmeric, paprika, chili pepper, and salt and pepper. Knead mixture with your hands. Store in a resealable plastic bag. Let stand and marinate in a cool area (cooler, or in a cold stream or snow bank) for 1 hour. If desired, prepare couscous or rice according to package directions. Let stand, keeping it warm.

Wet your hands and divide the meat mixture into egg-sized portions. Roll them between your palms and mold each one around a skewer in the shape of a sausage. The result will look a lot like a cattail. Place the skewers on a grill or over a fire and cook for about 8 minutes, turning regularly. Serve with couscous or rice. Serves 4.

* * * * * * * * * *

Corinne Humphrey is a food/travel writer and photographer whose other job as an international flight attendant allows her to wander the globe sampling what the world has to offer. She is the author of *Camping* (Golden Books Adult Publishing), and her articles and photos have appeared in *Cooking Light, Utah Outdoors, Sunset, Women's Health & Fitness,* and other publications. "My goal is to become an international food columnist," she says. "Eating, traveling, and talking — now that's *my* idea of a triathlon."

"When mariners are in trouble, they send out an SOS—Morse code for 'Save Our Ship.' When hungry campers clamor for SOS, it has a more relaxed meaning and doesn't involve life preservers or rescue by the Coast Guard. 'Stuff on a Stick' or kabobs, are perfect for outdoor grilling and turn any meal into a festive affair. Everyone becomes involved, as marinade mixers, food choppers,

or kabob builders. Because food is cut into chunks or strips, grilling times are minimal. Marinades can be made ahead of time and placed in resealable plastic bags with chunks of chicken, pork, or vegetables and then strung on skewers at the campsite, allowing everyone to customize his or her dinner.

"You can use either metal or wood skewers. If using metal ones, remember that heat will transfer through the middle of the food, cooking from the inside as well. Wood skewers should be soaked in water for at least 20 minutes to avoid burning."

See Corinne's recipe for Apple-Orange-Rum Compote, page 145

Good
Cont-

Buck Tilton

Wind River Spicy Shepherd's Pie

4 to 5 cups water
⅓ cup powdered milk
3 tablespoons butter or margarine
1 bouillon cube
2 cups instant potatoes
1 cup dried corn
1½ to 2 cups instant refried beans (or black beans)
2 tablespoons onion flakes
Salt and pepper, to taste
Tabasco sauce (optional)
1 cup cheese, cut into small bits

In a large pot, bring 2 cups water to a boil. Stir in milk, butter, and bouillon cube. Add potatoes to rehydrate. Let stand. In a frying pan, bring another 2 cups water to a boil. Add corn, beans, and onion. Simmer until corn and beans are rehydrated and tender, adding up to a cup more water, as necessary. Remove from heat. Spread potatoes over beans and corn. Add salt, pepper, and Tabasco (if desired). Top with cheese. Cover and bake on stovetop until hot, and cheese melts (about 15 minutes). Serves 3 to 4.

• • • • • • • • • •

Buck Tilton is cofounder of the Wilderness Medicine Institute of the National Outdoor Leadership School (NOLS). He has traveled extensively, far beyond the nearest restaurant, via foot, canoe, and sea kayak. Buck lives in Wyoming and is a regular contributor to *Backpacker* magazine.

"Call it the ordinary, the mundane, the everyday, the rut into which the wheels of life slip so easily, but know the common thread woven through them all: a lack of adventure. I agree completely with the ineffable Helen Keller, who wrote despite her physical blindness, 'Life is either a daring adventure or nothing.' The world opened to Ms. Keller because, day by day, she reached beyond the ordinary in search of the remarkable, the distinguishable. Ms. Keller opened to the world because she chose, in her own words, 'to behave like a free spirit in the presence of fate.' She climbed no earthly mountains, splashed down no turbulent rivers, sailed no distant salty seas. Yet, undoubtedly, her life was filled with adventure. She felt the surge of adrenaline when she stepped onto unknown mental and spiritual ground. Her heart soared, not necessarily with the last step up to a windswept summit, but with each footfall of her journey.

"Adventure, then, is a stretch of the mind, an expansion of the heart. Without adventure, life becomes a book with only one page. Without adventure, the human spirit withers, and then dies. 'Give me the storm and tempest of thought and action,' wrote Robert Ingersoll, 'rather than the dead calm of ignorance and faith!'

"The most tragic end of any life is an old man or woman sitting in a rocking chair in the sun's final rays muttering 'I could have' or 'I should have.'"

See Buck's recipe for Alaska Smoked Salmon Pasta, page 111.

Ted Millan

Old Goats' One-Pot Ginger Cashew Chicken Fried Rice

2 tablespoons olive oil
1½ cups dehydrated basmati rice
½ cup dehydrated jerked chicken*
2 tablespoons soy sauce
¼ to ½ tablespoon dried garlic, or garlic powder, to taste
¼ cup dehydrated green/red peppers
½ cup dehydrated broccoli
¼ cup dehydrated carrots
¼ cup dehydrated water chestnuts
¼ cup dehydrated scallions
3 cups water
¼ to ½ tablespoon ground ginger
Salt and pepper, to taste
1 chicken bouillon cube, crumbled
¼ cup dehydrated peas
½ cup dehydrated shiitake mushrooms
3 powdered or dehydrated eggs
½ cup cashews
2 tablespoons gourmet sauce (sweet Asian sauces, such as Mr.
   Yoshida's brand)

Place the oil, rice, chicken, 1 tablespoon soy sauce, and garlic in deep skillet or pot. Toss in the peppers, broccoli, carrots, water chestnuts, and scallions. Cover with 2 to 3 cups water (enough to cover). Add ginger, salt, and pepper to taste. Add the bouillon cube. Bring to boil. When the water boils, stir in peas and mushrooms. Cover and reduce heat to medium low. Simmer, stirring occasionally for about 20 minutes. Slowly stir in the powdered eggs. Add cashews, 1 tablespoon gourmet sauce, and a bit more ginger. Stir. Cover and cook another 10 minutes. Remove from heat, and stir in remaining soy and gourmet sauces. Replace cover. Keep warm until ready to eat. Serves 3 to 4.

* * * * * * * * * *

*If you dry your own food, marinate the chicken first with sweet Asian-flavor sauce. See "Ted Millan's Trail Food–Drying Basics," beginning on page 221.

"The Old Goats Patrol in our troop is comprised of the members who are over the age of 18, although most are much older than that. The younger Scouts

usually won't take the time to cook anything beyond instant soup, or they chow down on M&Ms, so this recipe is for the Old Goats of Troop 186 who appreciate fine dining. This is a nourishing, compact, lightweight, and spicy meal. It also has an extremely lengthy shelf life. Higher altitude doesn't retard cooking time. All ingredients can be prepackaged at home for ease of preparation."

See Ted's recipes for Angry Moose Scrambled Eggs, page 20 and Makemwait Mushrooms, page 90. "Ted Millan's Trail Food–Drying Basics" can be found beginning on page 221. His biography appears on page 90.

R. J. Secor

Vision Quest Refried Beans & Rice

1 cup instant rice
½ cup dehydrated refried beans
1½ cups water
1 packet taco seasoning mix
Parmesan cheese, grated, to taste
Red pepper or paprika, to taste
Wild onions, chopped (optional)

At home, mix together the rice and beans. Place in a resealable plastic bag. At camp, boil water. Pour rice mixture into a large cup or bowl. Stir in water. Cover and let stand about 5 minutes. Stir in taco mix, cheese, red pepper, and onions (if desired). Serves 1.

• • • • • • • • •

R.J. Secor of Pasadena, California, has been mountaineering for thirty-five years. He has attained coveted List Completion status twice in the Sierra Peaks Section of the Sierra Club, with more than 750 mountain ascents in the High Sierra in California and has summitted as many as sixty peaks in a single year. R.J. has also climbed extensively in other western states, British Columbia, Alberta, and Alaska. Other mountain adventures have taken him to the Himalaya in Tibet and Nepal, the Karakoram in Pakistan, the Andes in Argentina, and the volcanoes of Mexico. R.J. is the author of *The High Sierra: Peaks, Passes, and Trails* (The Mountaineers Books), *Mexico's Volcanoes: A Climbing Guide* (The Mountaineers Books), and *Aconcagua: A Climbing Guide* (The Mountaineers Books).

"I call my week-after-week hikes in the High Sierra 'Vision Quest.' One year I went on a thirty-day Vision Quest and cached some of my food in the bear barrel at a wilderness ranger station. When I returned to the station, the barrel was empty. Someone had taken my food! I had nine days left in my quest, yet I decided to continue, rationalizing that fasting was part of the Native American vision quest experience. I soon discovered that most of the John Muir Trail through-hikers carried too much food and were anxious to give some away. I received so much food that I finished the quest with a modest surplus!"

See R.J.'s recipe for Character-Assessment Gorp, page 69 and Coffee Can Cheesecake, page 144.

Sibylle Hechtel

Camp Four Curry

3 cups water
1 cup bulgur
1 fresh onion, chopped, dried onion flakes, or or ½ package
   onion soup mix
Indian curry powder
½ to 1 cup dry milk
1 6½-ounce can tuna
Dried fruit, to taste (raisins, figs, apricots, or peaches)
Peanuts, to taste
Coconut flakes

Bring water to a boil. Add bulgur, and boil for about 10 minutes. Add
the onion, curry, dry milk, tuna, and fruit. Boil 5 or 10 minutes longer,
or until bulgur is tender. Just before serving, stir in peanuts. Sprinkle
individual servings with coconut. Regular brown rice may be substituted
for the bulgur, but it takes longer to cook and doesn't taste as good.
Serves 2.

• • • • • • • • • •

Sibylle Hechtel is a freelance writer who lives in the Colorado Rockies,
overlooking Lake Dillon and the Gore Range. She has done many difficult
rock climbs, including a first ascent of Rainbow Wall in Red Rocks, Nevada, in 1988. In 1987, Sibylle was a member of the U.S.–Soviet mountaineering exchange to the Aksu range, one of the world's premier alpine
climbing areas, in what is known today as Kyrgyzstan. She was a member
of the Austrian women's Shishapangma expedition in 1994.

*"I was born in Stuttgart, Germany, to mountaineering parents, Richard and
Lisa Hechtel, who met while climbing. My father made many first ascents in
Europe and has climbed extensively in the United States and in other regions.*

*"I have done many Big Wall routes in Yosemite. On El Capitan, I did the Nose
Route in four days, the Salathe Wall in five, and the first all-woman ascent of the
Triple Direct, with Beverly Johnson, in seven days. Elsewhere in the Sierra Nevada, I did the Southwest Face of Conness in about ten hours, and the first free
one-day ascent of the East Face of Keeler Needle (the 14,240-foot summit just
south of Mount Whitney). I have done new routes on the North Face of Mount
Mitchell in Wyoming and on the West Face of Snowpatch Spire in the Bugaboos
of British Columbia and have climbed Mexico's three highest volcanoes.*

"Multiday climbs on Big Walls pose quite a weight problem. On the Triple Direct, Bev and I hauled the equivalent of our own weight—this included 56 pounds (7 gallons) of water, some 40 pounds of climbing hardware and equipment, and, of course, food. On wall climbs we don't take stoves because of the weight. For breakfast we usually have granola, and during the day we just eat gorp, maybe a salami or tuna sandwich, and a couple of cans of fruit—peaches, mandarin oranges, apricots, or plums."

Claudia Pearson

Mary's Fantastic Bulgur Pilaf

1 cup bulgur wheat
1 cup water
Vegetarian soup base (chicken-flavored bouillon cubes,
    powdered broth/stock, etc. work well)
1 teaspoon curry powder
1 teaspoon soy sauce (or more to taste)
½ teaspoon honey or other sweetener (brown sugar or maple
    syrup)
½ cup dried fruit, chopped
½ cup nuts and seeds (mix your choice)

Place bulgur in a large pot or bowl. Boil water. Stir in soup base. Pour soup mixture over bulgur. Add curry powder, soy sauce, honey, fruit, and nuts. Mix well. Set aside in cool area for at least ½ hour. The longer it sits, the more tender the pilaf. Serves 4.

• • • • • • • • • •

"This vegetarian version is geared toward backcountry cuisine. It can be made as a main or side dish with many possibilities for variation. Add canned chicken, fresh fish, cooked lentils, or sliced jerky for more protein. Season with hot sauce, Thai chili garlic sauce, fresh or powdered garlic, coconut, coconut milk, garam masala spice blend, or fresh herbs."

"Mary Howley Ryan MS, RD, who created this recipe, worked at National Outdoor Leadership School (NOLS) Rocky Mountain, for three seasons, conducting a nutrition study of all NOLS rations. She wrote the foreword and updated all of the nutrition information for the fifth edition of NOLS Cookery. If anyone can create a good recipe for bulgur, it's Mary!"

See Claudia's recipe for Donna's Gado-Gado Spaghetti, page 114, and Katie's No-Bake Energy Nuggets, page 49. Claudia's biography appears on page 49.

Chris Townsend

Scandinavian Macaroni

2 cups water
1 cup quick-cook macaroni (cooks in 5 minutes or less)
½ packet instant tomato soup mix (or 2 tablespoons tomato
   puree)
1 clove garlic, peeled and crushed*
1 tablespoon powdered milk (optional)
¼ cup grated cheddar or Parmesan cheese
Dried basil and oregano (or other herbs), to taste
Pepper, to taste

*You can substitute ⅛ teaspoon of garlic powder, but it doesn't taste as good.

Bring water to boil. Add macaroni and cook until tender. Do not drain.
Add soup mix, powdered milk, garlic, and herbs. Stir well. Remove from
heat. Stir in cheese and pepper. Serves 1.

• • • • • • • • • •

*"Scandinavian Macaroni gained its name on a three-and-a-half-month long,
1300-mile walk the length of the mountains of Norway and Sweden. I bought
food as I went along. Macaroni was the quickest-cooking base for a meal, so I
ate it nearly every night. I tried other types of soup mix, but tomato was definitely the tastiest. I won't say I got fed up with this meal, but I was certainly
happy not to eat it for a while, after I completed the walk."*

**See Chris's recipes for Ski Tour Chili Rice, page 112, and Ooey-Gooey
Flapjacks, page 57. His biography appears on page 57.**

Thomas F. Hornbein

Unmentionable Brew

4 cups water
1 to 2 packages soup mix (any flavor or combination)
Freeze-dried vegetables (peas, carrots, etc., any amount)
Dry minced onion, bean sprouts, etc., to taste
Freeze-dried hamburger (or other freeze-dried meat), broken
    up, to taste
Salt, pepper, curry, etc., to taste
Instant rice or instant mashed potatoes, etc. (optional)

Heat water. Add soup, vegetables, and meat in any flavor, combination, and amount. Add seasonings listed or a few other exotic condiments. At the stage of cooking indicated on the soup package directions (or use your judgment), enrich the brew (if desired) with rice, a small quantum of instant mashed potatoes, or other such stuff. The end result is a large molten mass of material anywhere between a moderately thick soup to something that would require an ice ax to disarticulate.

* * * * * * * * * *

Thomas F. Hornbein, M.D., of Bellevue, Washington, is professor emeritus of anesthesiology, physiology, and biophysics at the University of Washington. With Willi Unsoeld, he ascended the previously unclimbed West Ridge of Mount Everest and descended to the South Col, thus accomplishing a new route and the first traverse of the world's highest peak on May 22, 1963. The 1963 American Everest Expedition also placed four men on the summit via the South Col: James Whittaker, Nawang Gombu, Barry Bishop, and Luther Jerstad. *Everest: The West Ridge* (The Mountaineers Books) by Tom documents the new route and the traverse of the 29,028-foot Himalayan peak. In 1995, he climbed the Casual Route on the Diamond, East Face, Longs Peak, in Colorado. In 1996, forty-five years after his previous visit, Tom returned to Zumie's Thumb, East Face, Longs Peak, to carry Clerin Zumwalt's ashes. Today, he teaches, writes, and wanders and climbs moderate mountains in moderation (translated: more slowly).

"I have been active in mountaineering since 1944, particularly in the western United States. In 1957 I was on an expedition to then-unclimbed Mount Huntington in the Alaska Range (the 12,240-foot peak remained unclimbed until 1964, when the first ascent was made by a French party led by Lionel Terray). In 1960 I was on the American expedition to the Karakoram that

made the first ascent of 25,660-foot Masherbrum—Willi Unsoeld and George I. Bell climbed it July 6, and Nick Clinch and Jawed Akhter July 8.

"I don't really have much in the way of culinary input because my major single article of diet in the mountains is a rather large pot of this Unmentionable Brew. One beauty of this particular concoction is the fact that if you make enough at dinnertime, then all you have to do is heat the pot next morning and have more of same before taking off."

Buck Tilton

Alaska Smoked Salmon Pasta

4 garlic cloves
2 shallots
3 tablespoons butter
4 tablespoons dried tomato bits
1 envelope Herb-Ox instant chicken broth
Water
8 ounces dry smoked salmon
8 ounces angel hair pasta
¼ cup capers
Parmesan cheese, grated, to taste

Peel and chop garlic cloves and shallots. Lightly sauté in butter. Add dried tomato bits, chicken broth, and ½ cup water. Remove from heat, flake salmon into the mix, and let stand 15 to 20 minutes. Fill a pot with water and bring to boil. Add pasta and cook till done. Toss together pasta, salmon mixture, and capers. Sprinkle with Parmesan cheese. Serves 4.

* * * * * * * * * *

See Buck's recipe for Wind River Spicy Shepherd's Pie, page 100. His biography appears on the same page.

Chris Townsend

Ski Tour Chili Rice

2 cups water
½ cup quick-cooking rice
1½ cups dried vegetables (mushrooms, tomatoes, onions, and
    peas)
¼ cup textured vegetable protein granules (TVP)*
1 teaspoon chili powder (or more to taste)
1 clove garlic, minced or pureed
1 or 2 tortillas

*Textured vegetable protein (TVP) is a good substitute for ground beef
in dishes such as tacos, chili, and stews. Find it at natural food markets.

Soak the vegetables and TVP in 1 cup water for at least half an hour (or
according to package directions). Do not drain. Add rice, 1 cup water,
chili powder, and garlic. Cook until water is absorbed and rice is tender.
Eat with tortillas. Serves 1.

• • • • • • • • • •

*"This recipe can easily be multiplied for a larger crowd. If there are two stoves
and two pans, the rice can be cooked separately from the chili vegetables, which
is a good idea when preparing large amounts. The meal can be turned into
curried rice by substituting curry powder for chili powder.*

"Tortillas fit neatly into a 5-quart pot for carrying in the pack."

**See Chris's recipes for Ooey-Gooey Flapjacks, page 57, and Scandinavian
Macaroni, page 108. His biography appears on page 57.**

Jerry Johnson

Alaska Glop

Water (sufficient for cooking rice or noodles)
Noodles or rice (consult package directions for amount
    needed for 2 servings)
Hard sausage, cut up (or freeze-dried meat), to taste
Freeze-dried vegetables, to taste
Dry onion, minced or chopped
1 package gravy mix (any flavor)
Salt, pepper, oregano, and thyme, to taste
Margarine
Cheese, chopped or slivered
Dried egg mix or freeze-dried eggs

Heat water. Add noodles or rice (if instant rice is used, add toward end of cooking period). Add meat, vegetables, gravy mix, flavorings, and margarine. Boil till all ingredients are tender; stir occasionally to keep mix from sticking to bottom of pot. Shortly before serving, stir in enough cheese and powdered egg to thicken. Serves 2.

● ● ● ● ● ● ● ● ● ●

Jerry Johnson and his family live in Fairbanks, Alaska, where he is a senior scientist with the USA Cold Regions Research and Engineering Laboratory. He does research on the physics and mechanics of snow, ice, frozen ground, granular media, and the Martian polar regions. His work has taken him to Europe, Asia, Greenland, and all parts of North America, including the Arctic Ocean. These travels have given Jerry the opportunity to play in the mountains of France, Switzerland, and North America, where Alaska Glop still tastes good on cold winter trips.

"This glop really sticks to the ribs. The noodles or rice provide the bulk. The eggs and cheese thicken it and, with the margarine, turn it into a gourmet meal. Sausage is delicious and provides some of the extra fat needed in cold climates. The desire for fat in the diet determines the amount of margarine used. On climbs longer than one and a half or two weeks, it isn't uncommon for two people to need up to a quarter of a pound per meal. We used to enjoy this glop on Alaska climbing trips, and I still use it on my mountain outings in the Pacific Northwest."

Claudia Pearson

Donna's Gado-Gado Spaghetti

½ pound spaghetti (or 2 packages Ramen noodles)
4 cups water
3 tablespoons + 1 tablespoon vegetable oil
2 tablespoons sunflower seeds, raw and shelled
1 tablespoon dried onion, rehydrated
½ tablespoon or one packet broth
3 tablespoons brown sugar
1 teaspoon garlic powder
½ teaspoon pepper
½ teaspoon hot sauce (optional)
½ teaspoon spice (optional)
¾ cup water or more as needed
3 tablespoons vinegar
3 tablespoons soy sauce
3 tablespoons peanut butter
Green or wild onions, sliced (optional)

Bring water to boil. Add 1 teaspoon oil. Break pasta in half and put into boiling water. Cook until done; drain immediately and let stand. Over medium heat, in a frying pan, heat 3 tablespoons oil. Add sunflower seeds and onions. Stir for 2 minutes. Add broth, sugar, garlic, other spices if desired, and ¾ cup water. Stir in vinegar, soy sauce, and peanut butter. Do not burn! Serve sauce over pasta. Serves 3.

This dish can be fairly salty. For less saltiness, reduce or eliminate the broth, or use reduced sodium broth. The recipe is best cold and it loses some of its saltiness as it sits. Mix sauce and spaghetti, cool quickly, and serve chilled. If available, sliced green or wild onions add to the flavor.

• • • • • • • • •

This recipe was created by Donna Orr, coauthor of the second, third, and fourth editions of *NOLS Cookery*. Donna worked in the Rations Department for five years and now has another position at National Outdoor Leadership School (NOLS) Rocky Mountain.

See Claudia's recipes for Mary's Fantastic Bulgur Pilaf, page 107, and Katie's No-Bake Energy Nuggets, page 49. Claudia's biography appears on page 49.

Merrill Hayden

Poison Ivy Pesto with Shrimp

    8 to 12 ounces pasta (bowtie variety works well)
    8 to 12 ounces frozen shrimp (cooked and peeled)
    ½ cup pesto (frozen or refrigerated)
    6 to 7 sun-dried tomatoes
    Parmesan cheese, grated, to taste

At home, place the shrimp and pesto in separate resealable plastic bags. Keep shrimp frozen, and pesto refrigerated or frozen until just before you leave. At camp, heat two pots of water, bringing one pot to a boil. Add the sun-dried tomatoes to boiling water and cook for about 1 minute. Remove tomatoes from the water and add pasta. While the pasta cooks, chop the tomatoes into small pieces. To warm the pesto, briefly submerge the bag that contains the pesto into the pot of warm water (not boiling water). When the pesto is warmed, remove from the water. To warm shrimp, remove from the bag and add to the water. When the pasta is done, drain immediately. Remove shrimp from the water. Mix together the pasta, shrimp, pesto, and tomatoes. Sprinkle with Parmesan. Serves 2 to 3.

   This recipe is great for a first night out.

· · · · · · · · · ·

Merrill Hayden was born and raised in the San Francisco Bay Area. She did her first backpacking trip when she was ten years old, to Young Lakes

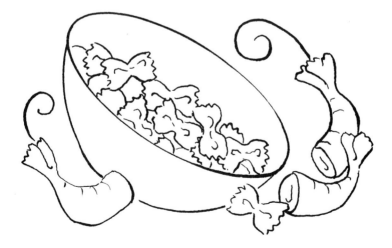

out of Tuolumne Meadows, in the high country of Yosemite. As she was growing up, she and her family backpacked in the Sierras and Mammoth Lakes areas. Merrill and her husband, Mike, moved to Idaho in 2000 and are now exploring the many backcountry areas around the state.

"My friend Rachel made this for us on a trip to Hells Canyon in eastern Oregon near the Idaho border. Being from northern California, I was familiar with poison oak, but had never seen poison ivy. On the drive to the trailhead, Rachel read from the hiking book that we should be on the lookout for poison ivy. We thought that was helpful advice, but didn't know what it looked like. Turns out we made camp in a patch of it. Soon, poison ivy attacked me—all over my body, including on my buttocks. Having it on the bottoms of my feet was the worst. For weeks after the trip, there were times when I'd have to drop what I was doing, yank off my shoes, and scratch wildly just to get some relief from the itching. I researched poison ivy on the Internet and have the image of the plant embedded in my brain. I won't make that mistake again!"

See Merrill's recipe for Quick & Easy Indian Dinner, page 126.

Guy Gosselin

Multitude-of-Sins Sauce

1 16-ounce can tomatoes
1 package onion soup mix
1 fresh onion, chopped
3 to 4 slices processed American cheese
Large pinch cinnamon
Salt and pepper, to taste
Walnuts or almonds (optional)
Cornstarch or flour to thicken
Old porridge, bread, or meat; or cooked rice, noodles, or
    instant mashed potatoes

In a pot, combine soup mix and tomatoes; simmer. Dice onion, and throw it into the pot along with the cheese. Add flavorings and nuts. Mix cornstarch or flour into cold water to make a thin paste, and stir enough into the boiling mixture to thicken it to near glacial consistency. Serve sauce over leftovers to cover up a multitude of sins. Or if you have two pots instead of only one, serve sauce over rice, noodles, etc., prepared according to package directions.

● ● ● ● ● ● ● ● ● ●

Guy Gosselin, a lifelong resident of Gorham, New Hampshire, used to spend two weeks a month on the summit of Mount Washington, the highest peak in the White Mountains, where he was director of the Mount Washington Observatory. He retired from the observatory in 1998.

"The observatory is a private nonprofit organization primarily devoted to scientific research and educational endeavors such as the summit museum. But it has had a lot to do with hikers and hiker safety over the years, including search and rescue, particularly in winter. The peak's elevation is only 6288 feet, but the top is approximately 3000 feet above timberline and lies in the path of three major tracks. It has some of the most severe and rapidly changing weather known outside polar regions—the climate on top is comparable to that of Labrador. Since records have been kept, its maximum temperature has never exceeded 72°F, and the lowest was 47°F below zero. As much as 49 inches of snow have fallen in a single day, and 566 inches in a year.

"But it is the wind that gives Mount Washington its claim to the world's worst weather. Velocities in excess of 75 miles per hour—hurricane force—occur on an average of 104 days a year; winds of 100 miles per hour are common in

winter and not unknown in summer. The mountain also holds the record for observed surface winds—231 miles per hour in April 1934. There are few, if any, other places in the world that have such high winds in combination with below-zero temperatures. Besides that, the summit is swathed in dense fog 60 percent of the time. No wonder hikers often find themselves in trouble."

Kristin Hostetter

Off-Piste Pesto Pasta

4 cups water
12 ounces dried pasta (your preference)
1 cup sun-dried tomatoes
2 cloves garlic, finely chopped
1 package Knorr pesto mix
¼ cup olive oil
¼ cup dried vegetables
¼ cup pine nuts (preferably toasted)
Parmesan cheese, grated, to taste

To a pot of boiling water, add pasta, tomatoes, garlic, and veggies. Cook until al dente. Drain all but a little bit of water (save the drained water for drinking, if you dare). Add pesto mix, olive oil, and pine nuts. Toss well and sprinkle with Parmesan cheese. Serves 4.

• • • • • • • • • •

"This is an impressive meal that everyone loves. It's my 'old standby' that gets served on every trip I take because it's easy, satisfying, and tough to beat in the taste department, especially when you sprinkle it liberally with Parmesan cheese."

See Kristin's recipes for Cascade Morning Couscous, page 19, and Rodeo Rice, page 92. Her biography appears on page 19.

Andy Selters

Cholatse Chowder

⅓ cup sun-dried tomatoes
1 bouillon cube, or instant soup powder
1½ cups water, more or less, to taste
⅔ cup potato pearls, or instant potato flakes
¼ cup instant dried beans
⅓ cup milk powder
1 tablespoon butter

Crumble the dried tomatoes and bouillon cube into water and bring to boil. In big mug or bowl, mix together potato pearls, dried beans, and milk powder. Pour the boiling soup mixture into the mug or bowl. Stir until it is the consistency of thick gravy. Add butter, stirring well. Cover and let stand for 3 minutes. Serves 1.

• • • • • • • • • •

Andy Selters of Bishop, California, is a long-time mountaineer, mountain guide, photographer, and cartographer. He has climbed extensively in North and South America and has established new routes in Pakistan and Nepal. Andy is the author of *Ways to the Sky* (The American Alpine Club) and *Glacier Travel & Crevasse Rescue* (The Mountaineers Books).

"I dove headfirst into mountaineering in my late teens. An ascent of the North Face of Mount Robson was an early personal breakthrough. I landed a job as a guide, which eventually took me to Alaska, Mexico, India, and Nepal. These trips allowed me to climb, trek, and bike on my own in those areas. I also undertook a number of technical climbing expeditions and a bike ride across southern Tibet. During the early 1990s I also helped lead cultural treks that raised money for secular and religious students in Ladakh, the culturally Tibetan area at the northern tip of India. In the Yukon I made the second alpine-style ascent of the north buttress of Mount Kennedy, but our flight out crashed, killing the pilot and badly breaking my back. After two years I've recovered pretty well. Now, with a wife and new son, I work as a freelance writer and photographer.

"Probably my most successful climbing trip was one that had me climb two new routes on Cholatse, a 21,128-foot-high peak in the Mount Everest area. My main partner on the climb was Tom Walter, a friend since college. For an alpine-style technical climb such as this, we wanted instant dinners but not necessarily freeze-dried. As an instructor for the National Outdoor Leadership School (NOLS), Tom had access to a variety of backcountry staples. It was his idea to mix potato

pearls, milk powder, and soup powder. Minutes after settling into our bivouacs we enjoyed great dinners. For years I wondered if perhaps the key ingredient had been a hard day of climbing at high altitude. But since then I've added the beans (cooked and dried myself), tomatoes, and butter, and successfully shared it with others during more pedestrian outings."

Paul Richins

Vegetable, Salmon, and Rice Dinner

3¼ cups water
1 package Knorr cream of broccoli soup (or other vegetable
    flavor)
½ cup powdered milk
1 cup instant rice
1 cup dried vegetables
1 6-ounce can salmon

Put water, soup, and milk into a pot. Stir while bringing to boil. Add rice, vegetables, and salmon. Stirring frequently, simmer 5 to 7 minutes, or until rice is done and salmon is heated thoroughly. Serves 2.

• • • • • • • • •

Paul Richins was raised in Weaverville, California, and started hiking, climbing, and backcountry skiing in the ruggedly beautiful Trinity Alps at the age of twelve. He has participated in numerous successful expeditions in Alaska, Canada, Tibet, Argentina, and Ecuador. In April 1991, along with two other climbers, Paul completed the first ascent of the Southwest Ridge of Stortind (Lyngen Alps, Northern Norway). He is the author of *Trekking California* (The Mountaineers Books), *Mount Whitney: The Complete Trailhead to Summit Hiking Guide* (The Mountaineers Books), and *50 Classic Backcountry Ski and Snowboard Summits in California* (The Mountaineers Books). Paul is an economist and lives in the Sierra Nevada foothills east of Sacramento, California.

"This recipe was developed by my sister, Judi Richins. Judi is a music and piano instructor in Northern California and has been backpacking in the Trinity Alps and Sierra Nevada for the past six years. For variety, add seasonings, onion flakes, or chunks of cheese to taste, if desired."

See Paul's recipes for Mushroom Garlic Chicken Dinner, page 134, and Sierra Slush, page 162.

J. Alex Maxwell

Glue Stew

3 to 4 cups water
Soup mix, any flavor
Dried vegetables or freeze-dried vegetables, to taste
1 12-ounce can corned beef, jerky, or freeze-dried meat
Salt, curry, or other strong flavorings to punch up taste

Reconstitute dried vegetables as time and type permit. Boil everything together. (For a truly traditional old-time flavor, give sufficient inattention to assure generous portions being scorched on the bottom of the pan.) When ingredients are reasonably tender (and all rodents for half a mile around have been spooked with its nutritious permeating odor), this glutinous glue is ready to eat.

● ● ● ● ● ● ● ● ●

J. Alex (Lex) Maxwell of Yakima, Washington, was a pioneer climber, backpacker, skier, and leader in mountain rescue work. Lex put up new routes on Mount Adams, Mount Stuart, Ingalls Peak, Kloochman Rock, and elsewhere in the Cascades. Besides climbing all the major peaks in the Cascades of Washington and Oregon, he made ascents in the St. Elias Range in Alaska, in the Bugaboos of British Columbia, and of 17,887-foot Popocatepetl in Mexico. In 2003, Alex celebrated his ninety-third birthday, and he is now retired from climbing and skiing.

"Glue Stew is a formula obtained in the pharmacy of the packsack. The original ingredients date back to the days of dehydrated foods, which were slow to reconstitute compared with modern freeze-dried varieties. This brew wasn't too bad in a base camp because you could let the ingredients soak overnight, but when you were on the move and had limited cooking time, the dried foods were generally pretty tasteless, and the outcome sometimes pretty awful.

"A version I particularly remember was dished up in the North Cascades. Bob McCall, Bob Swenson, my wife, Mary, and I came down off Clark Mountain and were preparing our leave-taking meal in a beautiful but rainy meadow. We fellows were huddled under our ponchos as we tossed remnants of our food into one last mixture that Bob Swenson was stirring with a stick. Mary joined us, looked suspiciously at our concoction, and said, 'What kind of soup is that?' Just then, a big green beetle nose-dived into the soup with an audible plop. Without losing a stroke of his stirring, Swenson flatly stated, 'This is split beetle soup'."

Ruth Mahre

Spike's Mountain Spuds

Water
Instant mashed potatoes
Instant gravy mix
Summer sausage, diced (or canned chicken)
Bell peppers (your choice of color), chopped, to taste
Salt and pepper, to taste

Adjust quantities according to number of servings desired and yields indicated on packages of instant potatoes and gravy. Prepare instant potatoes as directed on package, adding gravy mix. Stir in sausage and peppers. Salt and pepper to individual preference.

● ● ● ● ● ● ● ● ● ●

Ruth Mahre of Wenatchee, Washington, is an orthopedic physical therapist. She grew up ski racing at White Pass, Washington, and, in her teens, began mountaineering with her father, Dave "Spike" Mahre. She received her B.S. at the University of Nevada, Reno, while on a ski racing scholarship. She has guided for Rainier Mountaineering Inc. (RMI) and Summits Adventure Travel on Mount Rainier, Denali, Kilimanjaro, and in the Italian Dolomites.

"Mashed potatoes are a staple for RMI's expedition seminars. As a first-year guide, one of my main responsibilities was preparing meals. One night at Camp Muir I struggled with the potato mix-to-water ratio, which resulted in dry, burned spuds. Fortunately, our neighboring RMI group's senior guide, Phil Ershler, came to my rescue with extra hot water, which saved the batch. He remarked with a smile, 'They sure didn't hire you for your cooking skills, did they Mahre?'"

"My father, Dave 'Spike' Mahre, is to thank for the additions to the basic potato mix. He taught me this rendition on a climbing trip on Mount Sehale in the North Cascades in 2002. At the age of 75, he made the last rock scramble to the summit look easy…it must have been his years of making and consuming nutritious mountain meals!"

See Ruth's recipe for Sherpani Cookies, page 152. Her dad, David Mahre, has a recipe for High-Energy Fruit Bars on page 54.

Merrill Hayden

Quick & Easy Indian Dinner

Water
2 to 3 pouches of ready-to-eat Indian meals*
Couscous (enough to yield 3 servings)
Seasonings, to taste**

Heat water in one pot. Follow directions on Indian meal packages to heat. Follow directions on couscous package to prepare contents. Add seasonings if desired. Stir before serving. Spoon Indian mixture over couscous. Serves 2 to 3.

*One brand that is easy to find is Tasty Bite. Many supermarkets and health food stores carry a variety of flavors. Find them in the ethnic food or prepackaged dinners sections. Tasty Bite dinners are packaged in a heavy foil pouch that can be heated in hot water. Favorite flavors include Bombay Potatoes and Jaipur Vegetables. If supermarkets don't have this brand, they usually have others.

**Garam masala, an Indian spice blend, is great for seasoning rice, noodles, couscous, or beans.

● ● ● ● ● ● ● ● ● ●

"I don't know if it is the fresh air or the exertion, but when I am backpacking I crave tasty ethnic food. Since my husband, Mike, and I moved to Idaho we miss the wide variety of international foods that we ate in San Francisco and Seattle—Indian, Thai, and Vietnamese, for example. Mike came up with this simple and nutritious camping meal. This essentially is a one-pot dinner because the food 'cooks' in individual pouches, making cleanup from the meal a snap."

See Merrill's recipe for Poison Ivy Pesto with Shrimp, page 115. Her biography appears on the same page.

Pete Takeda

Noodles Plus

1½ packages instant Ramen noodles (with or without seasoning packets)
2 cups water
Combination of extras (for breakfast or lunch/dinner)*

Boil water. Add noodles. Stir in breakfast or lunch/dinner extras. Simmer 3 minutes. Serves 1 to 2.

*Breakfast Extras: Brown sugar and/or cinnamon, nuts, and dried fruit, to taste; or 2 tablespoons sweetened condensed milk

*Lunch/Dinner Extras: Squeeze margarine, jerky, salami, dried tofu, and seasonings, to taste

• • • • • • • • • •

Pete Takeda of Boulder, Colorado, is a senior contributing editor to *Rock and Ice* magazine and a contributor to *Sports Afield* and *Backpacker*. He is the author of *Pete's Wicked Book* (PrimeMedia) and *National Geographic Extreme Sports: Climb!* (National Geographic). Pete is a longtime member of the Marmot Design Board and a Marmot-sponsored athlete. As an internationally recognized rock, ice, and alpine climber, he travels the world. He's competed in the ESPN Winter X Games and climbed in Alaska, Canada, Iceland, Europe, Mexico, and Scotland.

"I spent six years living in Yosemite Valley—rock climbing. After that, I moved to Colorado and took up ice and alpine climbing. I noticed that I couldn't carry the usual heavy stuff—like those canned favorites that were my staple on big walls—in the mountains. Through trial and error, and advice from friends and books (like this one), my climbing partners and I came up with some high-calorie, satisfying, and simple one-pot menus. The process wasn't without its hitches. One time, Dave Sheldon and I came upon the idea to eat the potato recipe with olive oil as the fat provider. One of us had heard the idea somewhere and thought it valid. The result was like eating thick, soupy olive oil. That's when we switched to squeeze margarine. Squeeze margarine lasts forever without refrigeration and adds fat and flavor while keeping one-pot cleanup a breeze (less stickage).

"Ramen is a ubiquitous and cheap all-rounder. Asian rice noodles (sometimes called rice sticks) are great for those avoiding wheat or who desire a little variety.

Either is good for breakfast or lunch/dinner when mixed with the extras mentioned earlier. At home, I repackage ramen in resealable plastic bags, then add the extra dry ingredients. Sweetened condensed milk—carried in a squeeze tube—satisfies the sweet tooth at breakfast and dessert. Dried tofu, jerky, and salami can be eaten alone or used to add flavor, protein, and fat to any recipe. For the ultimate carbo-glop, add a handful of potato flakes and margarine to the noodle recipe."

Lloyd and Mary Anderson

Foil Stew

1 sliced carrot per person
1 sliced or diced potato per person
Onion, chopped, to taste
Ground beef, ¼ to ½ pound per person
Salt, pepper, and other seasonings, to taste

Place vegetables in center of 12-inch square of foil. Put meat and seasonings on top. Fold sides of foil up and over, then hem the foil across the top to seal well. This is a natural for cooking over a bed of coals when you can have a campfire. (It can also be cooked over a one-burner stove, by placing 1 foil packet at a time over low flame or inside a covered cooking pot.) After 25 to 30 minutes, remove the bundle from the heat and unfold the foil, which becomes a plate. Be sure to pack out the foil. (Use raw ground beef early on a trip, unless it can be kept frozen or at least cold.)

* * * * * * * * * *

The late Lloyd Anderson resided in Seattle, Washington. Beginning in 1929, he climbed more than 450 peaks. Nineteen were first ascents, including the South Tower of Howser Spire in the Bugaboos in 1941. Lloyd climbed in Mexico, Switzerland, Italy, Austria, Norway, and Japan, as well as in Canada and the United States.

In 1938 Lloyd and his wife, Mary, along with twenty-three fellow Northwest climbers, founded Recreational Equipment Inc. (REI). The group structured REI as a consumer cooperative to purchase high-quality ice

axes and climbing equipment from Europe because such gear could not be purchased locally. Soon, other outdoors people joined the co-op, and the range of outdoor gear was expanded.

"When an order arrived, it was a festive occasion. We would make a celebration of it by inviting our friends in for dinner. Opening the packages was like Christmas. On the advice of one of our friends, we soon established a cooperative. For several years we handled all the orders from our home. Then we moved into a grocery co-op near the Seattle waterfront, where we displayed two shelves of outdoor equipment among the groceries. Later we joined a nearby co-op gas station. Little by little we expanded and eventually became established on Pike Street in downtown Seattle. By then we weren't catering only to Northwest customers: our mail-order business was thriving, and we were shipping to outdoor people all over the United States, and in Canada, Mexico, and South America. In time we moved to still larger quarters. The business—from which Lloyd retired in 1971—now has retail outlets across the country."

Bob and Ira Spring

Quick Mountain Glop

3 to 4 cups water
1 package vegetable soup mix
Meat (jar chipped beef, small can corned beef, or other meat)
Instant mashed potatoes

Heat water, add soup mix, and cook till done, about 20 minutes. Turn off heat and add meat. Stir in enough potato to achieve desired consistency and to satisfy appetites. Serve at once. Serves 2 to 4.

● ● ● ● ● ● ● ● ● ●

The late Ira Spring, a photographer and author, was considered the god-father of Pacific Northwest hiking books, with over twenty-five titles to his credit, including *100 Classic Hikes in Washington* (with coauthor Harvey Manning; The Mountaineers Books) and *An Ice Axe, a Camera, and a Jar of Peanut Butter* (his autobiography; The Mountaineers Books). Ira received the Theodore Roosevelt Conservation Award in 1992. The Spring Family Trail Fund was established in 2000. It is dedicated to keeping hiking trails open for this and future generations of hikers in the state of Washington. For more information visit *www.springtrailtrust.org.*

Bob Spring and his late wife Norma worked together as a travel writer/photographer team, beginning in the mid-1960s. They wrote a number of travel books on Alaska and Russia. Exotic world travels took them to Panama, Mexico, Fiji, Tahiti, and Australia. Bob lives in Bellingham, Washington, near his family, and still takes photographs when weather and subjects oblige, prefaced by his famous phrase, "Just one more . . . "

"My most memorable experience with food was running out of it. Two other climbers and I were within sight of civilization after a two-week trek on the Juneau Icefield. Juneau was so close that we could see cars moving on the streets below. There was no question, we would be down there the next morning for breakfast. At what should have been our last camp, we had a big meal of the remaining food and squandered the rest of our gas drying socks. All that was left were six prunes, a jar of jam, two raisins, and an empty stove. However, that night it rained and turned cold, and the small cliff we had to descend was solid ice. It took all day to go a quarter-mile, and we were stuck out another night, this time without heat to melt snow. We divided the prunes, two for each person, and made a large pot of ice cream with jam and snow. We couldn't figure out how to divide the two raisins three ways, so we flipped for them and I won both."

Helga Byhre

Helga's Stew

3 to 4 cups water (adjust according to soup package directions,
   and to taste)
1 package Maggi or Knorr soup mix (any flavor)*
Instant rice or instant mashed potatoes
Dried meat, to taste
Dried vegetables, to taste
Seasonings, to taste

*Maggi and Knorr brands seem to have more body than others.

Heat water. Stir in soup, meat, and vegetables. Add rice or potatoes at
the cooking time indicated on package. Stir well. Cook until all ingredients are tender. Add seasonings. Serves 2.

Variation: Rather than using soup mix with rice or potatoes, use prepared pasta or rice dinner mixes. Generally one package serves 2.

● ● ● ● ● ● ● ● ● ●

Helga Byhre of Shoreline, Washington, has been a climber and skier all
her life. She was born in Berlin, Germany. She spent some of her youth in
Switzerland, where she became "hooked on mountains." After immigrat-
ing to North America, she spent several years in Alaska, including one
year in a homemade log cabin in the Brooks Range. Helga remembers
her years in Alaska as the most beautiful of her life. Today, she travels all
over the globe; has substituted hiking, scrambling, and kayaking for climbing, but she still skis.

*"In Alaska, the only way to get to certain base camps in the mountain ranges is
by air. In the early 1960s, when I lived in Alaska, famous bush pilots Lowell
Thomas, Jr. and Don Sheldon were kept busy during climbing season, taxiing
climbers to and from these locations. To get to Denali, Don shuttled climbers to
a base camp located on a glacier.*

*"A year after my own attempt at that mountain, a party from Germany came
to climb two mountains to the west of McKinley. Due to bad weather, they had
to camp for about a week in Sheldon's hangar at Talkeetna. They were quite
restless when the weather finally cleared. The leader of the group, who didn't
speak English, took off with Don in his two-seater Super Cub. Upon arrival at
the glacier, the leader, let's call him 'Helmut,' realized that the bag containing
his food had been left behind. He attempted to communicate that to Don, but*

the latter interpreted that the German seemed excited to be in such a beautiful place. Upon returning to Talkeetna, Don learned the reality about the missing food, but the weather socked in for another five days! When it finally cleared, and just before he took off, Don rushed into his small house, grabbed a frying pan, complete with a cooked steak, from the stove. After taxiing to the camp on the glacier, Don jumped out of the airplane, handed Helmut the frying pan and steak and said, 'I am so sorry!'"

Paul Richins

Mushroom Garlic Chicken Dinner

3 to 3½ cups water
1 small zucchini, sliced
½ carrot, thinly sliced
Dried mushrooms
3 cubes garlic chicken bouillon
1½ packages instant Ramen noodles (with or without seasoning
    packets)
1 5-ounce can chicken
Salt and pepper, to taste

Bring water to boil, add zucchini, carrots, and mushrooms. Cook for 1 minute. Stir in bouillon, ramen (and seasoning, if desired), and chicken. Simmer 3 minutes or until noodles are done. Season with salt and pepper. Serves 2.

● ● ● ● ● ● ● ● ●

"This recipe was developed by my sister, Judi Richins. Judi is a music and piano instructor in Northern California and has been backpacking in the Trinity Alps and Sierra Nevada for the past six years."

See Paul's recipes for Vegetable, Salmon, and Rice Dinner, page 122, and Sierra Slush, page 162. His biography appears on page 122.

Mike Colpitts

Mountain Sushi

Water
3 cups uncooked rice (short- or medium-grain)
Seasoned rice vinegar, to taste
Condiments (sardines, salmon, pickled ginger, wasabi, etc.),
  to taste
Sesame seeds, to taste
Strips of omelet, mushrooms, bacon bits, etc., to taste
Nori (dried seaweed sheets), or inarizushi-no-moto (seasoned
  fried bean curd)

Cook rice according to package directions. Spoon into bowl and sprinkle with vinegar. Fluff rice with fork and "hand fan," so that steam and vinegar are absorbed, and it cools quickly. Add more vinegar to taste. Rice should be tasty but not soggy. If you are using nori, form rice into small palm-sized balls and sprinkle with condiments.

To eat, wrap the rice ball at the last moment with a strip of nori. If prepared and wrapped ahead of time, the nori will become soggy, so wrap rice/condiment balls and nori separately. If you are using inarizushi-no-moto, add toasted sesame seeds to seasoned rice. Open can or package of inarizushi and gently stuff rice into the pockets. Yields 25 to 30 balls.

• • • • • • • • • •

Mike Colpitts, M.D. of Seattle, Washington, is a climber and snowshoer who particularly enjoys alpine off-trail adventures in the Cascades. He spent six months in Nepal, living and working at Sir Edmund Hillary's Kunde Hospital for Sherpas at around 14,000 feet elevation in the Everest area. Sushi continues to be the mainstay in Mike's family's mountain diet, and is also a hit at soccer games and cross-country meets.

"The Sherpas don't measure distances the way we do—they use time instead of mileage to describe the distance from one point to another. If you were in very good physical condition, you could walk from the hospital to the Everest Base Camp in a day. When I worked there, we had two basic food courses: rice with potatoes on top, and potatoes with rice on top. We had a gourmet cook, but he could never get the ingredients for fancy foods. However, he did have a gourmet cookbook beautifully illustrated in color, and quite often before a meal I would look longingly at those pictures. It showed me how wrapped up in food we Americans are.

"For myself, I like to fast on one-day mountain trips. Going without eating for several hours provides an experience to push back my psychological limits. If I should ever find myself stranded without food for a day or more, it wouldn't be impossible for me to survive comfortably. In fact, a few years ago when I was on the way with a friend to climb Mount Rainier's Liberty Ridge, I discovered at our campsite that I had forgotten my food. I declined my friend's offer to share his and made the climb and descent without eating. I was a little short on energy, but made the climb in good shape."

Mary Staley

Icicle Canyon Sandwiches

French rolls
Butter
Lunch meat of choice
Corned beef (cooked at home or canned)
Cheese

At home, slit open rolls. Butter them well. Fill with generous amounts of sandwich meat, corned beef, and cheese. Wrap in aluminum foil. Keep refrigerated or frozen till you leave on trip. Keep as cool as possible during transport. At camp, drop the foil-wrapped bundles on the coals of a campfire if a campfire is permitted. That's the best cooking method, but the sandwiches can also be heated one at a time over a pressure stove with the flame turned low. Turn the foil packages occasionally. When the sandwiches are hot, remove bundles from the heat, open foil, and eat. Each sandwich makes a complete meal for one person. Serve with water, coffee, or a fruit drink.

· · · · · · · · · ·

Mary Wilson Staley of Quincy, Washington, began climbing in the early 1950s with the outing club at Washington State College (now Washington State University) at Pullman. The group made trips to the Cashmere Crags, an extensive rock-climbing area of fine granite spires on the east side of the Cascades in the vicinity of Icicle Creek and its tributaries. The Cashmere Crags were described by Ralph S. Widrig in the 1949 *American Alpine Journal* as "tall, threatening spires that streak skyward like Dantesque flames." Today Mary has seventeen grandchildren with varied talents and activities, including hiking and rock climbing. They keep life busy and interesting.

"I was the first woman to scale The Lighthouse, a tall isolated tower that had first been climbed in 1948 by Fred Beckey, Pete Schoening, and Widrig. The next year I returned to the Crags with the Cascade Crag Climbers, a Wenatchee-based club, for an ascent of Boxtop, a minaret-type summit on the Mount Temple ridge. (We turned back one rope length from the summit.) On that peak we were benighted and had a very tasty evening meal of whole wheat snack crackers spread with a mixed glob of peanut butter and honey. Icicle Canyon Sandwiches are among my camping standbys. They made many a hearty meal for my husband, Gene, and our four children."

John Simac

Schurman Hut Ham-And-Rice

2¼ cups water
7 ounces instant rice
2 ounces freeze-dried peas

1 6¾-ounce can ham
Seasonings, to taste

Bring water to boil. Add rice and peas. Simmer for 3 minutes, stirring to prevent sticking; add more water if needed. If freeze-dried ham is used, reconstitute according to package directions. Add ham to rice-pea mixture, reheat (stirring well), and serve. Serves 2.

John Simac of Tacoma, Washington, has climbed Mount McKinley and was on the first official winter ascent of Mount Rainier in 1965. His many contributions in the field of mountain rescue work include developing a backpackable hydraulic winch and helping develop the "storm kit" produced by the Tacoma Mountain Rescue Unit.

John was one of the prime builders of Schurman Hut, constructed between 1958 and 1962 at the base of Steamboat Prow on the north side of Mount Rainier. The hut, at 9500 feet elevation and about 5000 feet above the roadhead, serves not only as a high camp for climbers ascending the peak by the Emmons Glacier, but also as an emergency shelter in case of storm or accident. During the construction period, John climbed to this site at least 135 times, to carry materials and assist in building the shelter.

Our days were so full and time so short that we often brought a good, nourishing, home-cooked stew that could just be heated up for dinner. One evening, when the weather was extremely cold, our non-pump-type stove kept going out—very trying to our patience. At long last, the stew began to simmer. Holding the pot lid in one hand and a spoon in the other, with a flashlight tucked between chin and chest so I could see into the pot, I began to stir. The flashlight slipped and fell into the stew. The pot became top-heavy and tipped over—and the entire dinner spilled over onto the pumice. All those cold, tired, hungry, hard-working climbers had to go to bed without.

"Later in the project, Lee Tegmer, Max Eckenburg, and I were on the team that stayed to the finish of the cabin, and were the only team that had a five-woman group—referred to as "the harem." Without these women, it would have taken at least two more years to complete the project. Our food was first class, cooked on a two-burner Coleman stove."

Esther Courtney

Chelan Corned Beef Hash

1 12-ounce can corned beef
Chopped fresh onion (or equivalent dried), to taste
Seasonings, to taste
Hash brown potatoes (freeze-dried, or about half a 6-ounce
    package precooked dehydrated)

In a frying pan, cook meat, onion, and seasonings. Rehydrate potatoes in hot water, according to package directions; drain if necessary. Add potatoes to meat. Stir and cook till thoroughly mixed and well done. Serves 2.

● ● ● ● ● ● ● ● ● ●

Esther Courtney and her husband Ray (both deceased), lived in a two-story log house on the Stehekin River, just outside the North Cascades National Park boundary and nine miles north of Stehekin Landing. The isolated town of Stehekin, Washington, located in a national recreation area, is at the head of fifty-mile-long Lake Chelan and can be reached only by boat, small plane, or mountain trail.

Esther walked thousands of miles over trails that lead in and out of Stehekin. She was also a guide and cook for hiking trips in the North Cascades.

"In winter Ray and I both lead cross-country ski trips. Summers, Ray conducts pack trips by horseback into surrounding mountain areas, and I lead trips for people who like to hike without carrying heavy packs. Tents, supplies, and food go along by horse. Our sons and daughter all assist in the family business.

"For our trips I bake the bread we use, in my wood-burning range. I also plant a large garden—with a high fence to keep the deer out—and grow most of the vegetables used. Other food and supplies must be ordered well ahead, since it is a fifty-mile, two-day round trip by boat to the nearest supermarket. My hikers also come by boat. I often rendezvous with them at jumping-off points into the wilderness. They usually arrive hungry!

"On the trail, lunch frequently consists of peanut butter and jelly sandwiches, summer sausage, cheese, gorp, a fresh orange, and either water or a grapefruit or orange-flavored instant drink. Another dinner that is simple and delicious is made from macaroni, prepared according to package directions, with a large amount of grated cheddar stirred in; the cheese melts and forms a nice thick sauce. I do the cooking; but once a trip begins, I never have to wash a dish— my guests won't let me."

Grand Finale: Desserts

*I*f you like to indulge in desserts at home, there is no reason to do without them in your trail menu. Desserts are delightful treats that top off an exhilarating day and convivial dinner!

The recipes here are meant to satisfy. Some are made entirely at home and ride in your pack, and others are easy to whip up while dinner is cooking. From the classic Italian tiramisu to apple dumplings, and from s'mores bars to a creamy pudding, backcountry adventurers share their favorites.

Also, take another look at the chapter "Energizing Snacks, Breads, and Lunches," beginning on page 47. In it you'll find some delectable coffee cakes and other sweet calorie boosters that do double-duty as desserts.

Just remember . . . leave the guilt at home!

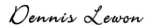

Trail Tiramisu

⅓ cup water
2 teaspoons instant espresso
2 tablespoons Kahlua
3.4 ounce package chocolate instant pudding mix
2 cups milk, from powder
16 ladyfingers
2 tablespoons cocoa or chocolate shavings

Bring water just to boiling point. Stir in espresso and Kahlua, mixing well. Prepare pudding according to package directions. Layer half the ladyfingers on bottom of a pot or deep dish. Drizzle ladyfingers with half the espresso mixture. Spread half the pudding over the top. Repeat with another layer of ladyfingers, espresso, and pudding. Sift cocoa or sprinkle chocolate shavings over the top. Chill dish in snow or cold water before serving. Serves 4.

• • • • • • • • • •

Dennis Lewon of Emmaus, Pennsylvania, is the equipment editor at *Backpacker* magazine. He has whipped up backcountry meals from Alaska to India to the Solomon Islands. He says his most challenging kitchen duty came as a wilderness guide for kids, when he learned how to cook for the world's most finicky eaters.

"Goodbye s'mores, hello Italy! The first time I made Trail Tiramisu was in Utah's Paria Canyon. It was the pièce de résistance during a friendly cook-off with friends. Of course, the overall effect of the dessert was helped by the ambience—a beach-front campsite along the Paria River, fiery sandstone walls lit by the setting sun, and balmy desert weather. To cap things off, I served this unbeatable dessert with a rich, dark ten-year-old port. It's not for zealots who pack ultra lightweight, but for everyone else this dish is a winner. For true espresso aficionados, pack a mini espresso maker and brew the fresh stuff!"

See Dennis's recipe for Canyon Crostinis, page 89.

R. J. Secor

Coffee Can Cheesecake

1 package no-bake cheesecake mix (flavor of your choice)
1½ cups water
Powdered milk to yield 1½ cups, when reconstituted

At home, place cheesecake mix packet in a resealable plastic bag. If mix includes fruit topping, place it in the same plastic bag. (Leave the crust mix packet at home—or place the crumbs in your bird feeder.) At camp, before preparing dinner, pour water and powdered milk into a 1-pound coffee can, with lid (or a large, wide-mouth Nalgene bottle, or a plastic container). Shake container to mix powdered milk and water. Add cheesecake mix. Shake vigorously for at least 3 minutes. Chill in snow, or cold stream, for at least one hour. Spoon into bowls or cups. Serve with fruit topping, if desired. Serves 4 to 6.

● ● ● ● ● ● ● ● ● ●

See R.J.'s recipes for Vision Quest Refried Beans & Rice, page 104, and Character-Assessment Gorp, page 69. His biography appears on page 104.

Corinne Humphrey

Apple-Orange-Rum Compote

6 cups cooking apples, chopped (about 2 pounds)*
1 8-ounce package mixed dried fruit pieces
¼ cup sugar
2 teaspoons shredded orange peel
¾ cup orange or apple juice
3 tablespoons rum (optional)
2 tablespoons quick-cooking tapioca
¾ cup sliced almonds or chopped walnuts
Whipped cream or yogurt, to taste (optional)

Combine apples and fruit pieces, sugar, orange peel, juice, rum (if desired), and tapioca in pot. Cover and cook over medium heat for 15 to
20 minutes. Serve sprinkled with nuts and with whipped cream or yogurt on the side, if desired. May also be served over couscous with milk
for a more filling dessert. Serves 10 to 12.

*You can substitute dried apple slices. Soak them ahead of time in water,
fruit juice, or rum to plump and soften.

· · · · · · · · · ·

*"On my birthday last year, a group of friends led me on my first all-day trek up
Mount Timpanogos near Salt Lake City, Utah. Just over the summit, we passed
a herd of mountain goats nibbling on spring grasses, and we realized how
hungry we were—time for us to think about grazing too. After chowing down
on salami sandwiches, Bill reached deep into his knapsack and pulled out one
whole intact cherry pie, six miniature cartons of milk, and singing candles
(yes, you can find candles that sing!) in honor of my birthday.*

*"While the idea of cherry pie a la mode at 11,000 feet is unique and fun, there
are other desserts that are more easily packed, nutritious, or more fulfilling
than a home-baked pie. Considering that a vigorous hiker burns 250 to 300
calories per hour, it pays to give even your desserts careful attention."*

**See Corinne's recipe for Moroccan Keftas, page 98. Her biography ap-
pears on the same page.**

Jon Van Zyle

Five-Pound Fudge

1 13-ounce can evaporated milk
4 cups sugar
3 4-ounce bars sweet baking chocolate, broken into small
  pieces
1 18-ounce package chocolate chips or morsels
1 7-ounce jar marshmallow creme
¼ cup (⅛ pound) butter or margarine
1 to 2 cups walnuts or pecans, toasted and chopped

Bring milk and sugar to boil in a very large saucepan. Stirring constantly, simmer at the boiling point for 7 minutes. Remove from heat, then quickly add sweet chocolate, chocolate chips, marshmallow creme, and butter. Stir until chocolate is dissolved and ingredients are well mixed. Add nuts. Pour into a buttered pan or casserole, and cool. Refrigerate for 8 hours before cutting. For variety, sprinkle the nuts over the top of the fudge as it cools, instead of stirring them in.

● ● ● ● ● ● ● ● ● ●

Jon Van Zyle, of Eagle River, Alaska, is an artist and outdoorsman. He and his wife Jona (also an artist) travel extensively, gathering material and experiences for their art. Jon has twice completed the 1049-mile-long Iditarod Trail Sled Dog Race between Anchorage and Nome. In 1979 he was made Iditarod artist, a title he still holds. In March 2004, Jon was inducted into the Anchorage Daily News Iditarod Hall of Fame. His acrylic paintings go beyond the race, and encompass Alaska's beauty, Native traditions, and history.

"Through the years I have viewed and absorbed the splendor of pristine landscapes from one end of the state to the other—the real Alaska: now-vanished villages with their silent totem poles telling tales of a forgotten era and people, forest-bordered lakes, abandoned line shacks, the stark loneliness of the northern frontier.

"I have always had dogs, and my wife, Charlotte, and I raise registered Siberian huskies. I have twice raced my dogs in the Iditarod dogsled races from Anchorage to Nome, a distance of 1150 to 1500 miles across the interior of Alaska. Strict rules govern the race—there are twenty-four checkpoints—and the trail is a testing ground for all kinds of things. The race usually takes two to four weeks. The racers are outdoors the whole time in temperatures that, with

the wind chill factor, can range from 40°F to 80°F below zero or lower. When you are racing a sled, you run about 40 percent of the time. For both training and racing, you need snack food that is extremely high in energy and light in bulk. This snack, coupled with good nutritional protein and high-calorie food, sustains a good diet."

Jane Wentworth

Comfort Pudding

3 tablespoons cornstarch	2 cups cold water
½ cup instant powdered milk	3 tablespoons cocoa powder, or ¼ cup white chocolate or butterscotch chips
2 to 4 tablespoons sugar	
½ teaspoon vanilla powder	
1 small cinnamon stick	

At home, mix together the dry ingredients. Store the mixture in a resealable plastic bag. Store cocoa powder or chocolate or butterscotch chips in a separate resealable plastic bag. At camp, place the dry mixture into a saucepan. Slowly add up to 1 cup cold water to the mix, stirring to make a smooth paste. Add another cup cold water. Heat, stirring constantly, until the mixture thickens. Stir in cocoa (or the chocolate or butterscotch chips) during the final minute of cooking, until melted and mixed thoroughly. Serves 2.

• • • • • • • • • •

Jane Wentworth of Bainbridge Island, Washington, is a botanist, native plant enthusiast, and champion against non-native invasive weeds. She enjoys hiking, sea kayaking, gardening, cooking, and traveling. Jane and her husband Keith have traveled and camped in various parts of Southeast Alaska, the Queen Charlotte Islands, Vancouver Island, the Canadian Rockies, Costa Rica, and New Zealand.

"I love to cook, and I enjoy tasty and nutritious food. As a backpacker, early on I was forever trying to come up with satisfying meals that were easy, lightweight, and didn't taste like cardboard. Imagine my delight upon discovering the possibilities afforded by being able to carry more in a sea kayak than I would dare carry on my back! Although I still love backpacking, kayak camping expanded my outdoor cooking repertoire to include things like baking in a Dutch oven and Greek salads that keep without refrigeration for several days.

"I adapted Comfort Pudding from a recipe that I found in the Puget Consumer's Cooperative (PCC) Natural Markets' newsletter years ago. While not entirely original, it is one of my favorite desserts when camping out because it's easy and yummy. The butterscotch or white chocolate versions are my own idea, for those of us who can't sleep after eating cocoa."

See Jane's recipe for Sweet & Spicy Moroccan Stew Over Couscous, page 93.

Mrs. F.D. (Harriet) Mack

North Star Ginger Dumplings

2½ cups water
4 ounces dried apples
Sugar, to taste
½ of a 14-ounce gingerbread mix
Just enough water to make a stiff dough (about ¼ cup)

Cook dried apples with water and sugar till they are tender. Make sure the applesauce is wet enough so it won't scorch during further cooking. Make a stiff (not runny) batter by combining the gingerbread mix with about half the water called for on the box for the proportion of mix used. With a large spoon, drop globs of dough onto the bubbling applesauce. Place lid tightly over pot and simmer for about half an hour (it may take longer at a high elevation). Dumplings rise in the steam, so don't peek under the lid until the specified time has passed. Serve as is, or add anything else you have, such as nuts, shaved chocolate, berries, or canned fruit.

• • • • • • • • • •

The late Mrs. F.D. (Harriet) Mack—"Rick" to her friends—lived in Sunnyside, Washington, before her death in 1980. Mrs. Mack had started her hiking career more than sixty years earlier by helping her husband with Boy Scout affairs. In the years following her first outings, she hiked alpine trails in the Cascades, Olympics, Sierra Nevada, Rockies, and the Swiss Alps; among the fjords of Norway; in the Himalaya of Nepal; and in Patagonia.

"A few years ago I figured out that for fifty years I averaged about 350 miles a year of backpacking, with a total of some 17,500 miles; and I spent at least a thousand nights on the ground in a sleeping bag. I took up skiing after I became a grandmother, and thereafter skied extensively in the North Cascades and elsewhere.

"I invented Ginger Dumplings in the late 1940s, when I was ski touring with friends in the North Cascades west of Lake Chelan. For five weeks we had skied, backpacked, and camped out nightly on deep snow. But none of us was quite ready to end our trip, even though food supplies had dwindled to a package of gingerbread mix and a sack of dried apples. Nobody was sure what to do with that combination. But I felt I would think of something, so I told the others to start the fire and make camp while I got the dinner. The result was far more delectable than some of the things we had mixed together according to plan. I named the recipe after North Star Mountain opposite our campsite."

June Fleming

S'Mores Bars

12 to 14 marshmallows, cut into several pieces each
1 cup chocolate chips
¼ pound graham crackers, crushed
1 to 2 tablespoons butter or margarine

Use a microwave oven or double boiler to melt marshmallow pieces and chocolate chips. Stop the melting process when you still see some marshmallow bits. Stir crushed graham crackers into the marshmallow/chocolate "goo." If goo is too stiff, add a bit of butter or margarine. Spoon mixture into greased pan, cut into bars, then chill.

● ● ● ● ● ● ● ● ● ●

"These days when hikers aren't very likely to have campfires, some of us miss the comfort of old-fashioned s'mores. You can combine the three basic ingredients at home in the form of bars. Shut your eyes when you eat them, and you will relive your childhood."

See June's recipes for Protein Power Muffins, page 34, Trail-Happy Salad, page 81, and Trail Coffees, page 160. Her biography appears on page 34.

Read S'More's lore on page 230.

H. Adams Carter

Wind River Ice Cream

Dry whole milk
Strawberry jam
Corn snow (or any other snow of mixable texture)

Stir milk, jam, and snow together in any amounts or proportions, to the desired flavor and consistency. This makes a delectable dessert or snack.

• • • • • • • • • •

The late H. Adams (Ad) Carter of Milton, Massachusetts, was a mountaineer of long and extensive experience. He climbed his first peak, Mount Washington in New Hampshire, in 1919, when he was five years old. In 1936 he was a member of the British-American Himalayan Expedition that made the first ascent of 25,645-foot Nanda Devi in Uttar Pradesh in northern India. Forty years later, Ad returned to Nanda Devi as coleader with Willi Unsoeld (now deceased) of an expedition jointly sponsored by the American Alpine Club and the Indian Mountaineering Federation. This expedition made the fifth ascent of Nanda Devi via a new route, the Northwest Face and North Ridge. Throughout the 1980s, he led numerous expeditions to the Cordillera Blanca in Peru, and he climbed extensively in numerous other areas, including Alaska. For many years, Ad was the editor of *The American Alpine Journal,* published annually by the American Alpine Club.

"On my first expedition to Alaska, in 1933, our food was pretty awful. It was far from nourishing, and there was never enough of it (I actually developed a mild case of scurvy toward the end of the trip). One day when we were storm-bound in the tent, we decided to pass the time by playing cards—for high stakes! The most valuable thing we could think of was our ration of powdered milk for one day.

"We played cards all day, and by evening I had cornered the entire ration of whole milk, sugar, and cocoa for all six of us. I envisioned the best, creamiest cup of cocoa that anyone ever had. While the others watched with their mouths watering, I mixed up the milk and the powdered cocoa. Next I grabbed the pressure-top can in which we kept the sugar and heaped in the sweet stuff. Hot water completed the ambrosial drink. Ecstatic with anticipation, I gulped a mouthful—and spat it right out. One of my companions had carefully emptied out the sugar and put salt in the can instead."

Ruth Mahre

Sherpani Cookies

2 cups flour, sifted
1 teaspoon baking soda
½ teaspoon baking powder
½ teaspoon salt
½ cup margarine or butter
¾ cup white sugar
¾ cup brown sugar
2 eggs
1 to 2 teaspoons vanilla
2 cups old-fashioned rolled oats
6 ounces chocolate chips

In a medium bowl, mix flour, baking soda, and salt. Set aside. In a large bowl, cream margarine and sugars. Beat in eggs and add vanilla. Mix the contents of the medium bowl into the contents of the large bowl. Stir in oats and chips. Drop by teaspoonfuls, about 1 inch apart, onto ungreased cookie sheets. Bake at 350°F for 10 to 13 minutes, or until lightly browned. Cool completely. Makes about 4 dozen cookies.

Variations: Rather than bake individual cookies, spread cookie dough into a 9 x 13-inch pan and bake at 350°F for 15 to 18 minutes. Cool then cut into squares. Or, substitute raisins for chips, and add 1 teaspoon cinnamon.

"I grew up on a variation of these cookies (the original called 'Cowboy Cookies'), thanks to my mother, Mary Mahre. She packed these for me to take on long ski racing trips. My teammates were thrilled when I shared. We found that there is nothing like a homemade cookie to lift the spirits. After all, just as climbing and skiing are truly 'foods for the soul,' the same is true with homemade baked goods!

"We have another family tradition, started by my sister, Kathee Forman, for outdoor adventure food—Ritz Cracker, Cheddar Cheese, and Cucumber Sandwiches. Pack crackers, cheese, and cucumber in separate containers. When you're ready for a snack, layer one cracker, one cheese slice, and one cucumber slice—or eat separately. These ingredients quench the desire for salt and moisture, while providing a source of energy—for hot summer day hikes. Cucumbers are great in sandwiches, because they are juicy and don't wilt like lettuce. Kathee can cut the cheese and cucumbers into the exact, consistent width for the ultimate taste outcome. Therefore, I always try to go hiking with her!"

See Ruth's recipe for Spike's Mountain Spuds on page 125. Her biography appears on the same page. See recipes for Peach Fluff Cake, page 60, and Blueberry Buckle, page 62, by Kathee Forman, Ruth's sister.

Eric Prater

Ugly But Good Chocolate Chip Cookies

2¼ cups flour (½ whole wheat and ½ white)
1 teaspoon baking soda
1 teaspoon salt
1 cup butter, softened (do not substitute margarine)
¼ cup granulated sugar
¾ cup brown sugar (packed)
1 teaspoon vanilla
2 large eggs
1 to 1¼ cup chocolate chips
½ to ¾ cup nuts, chopped (optional)

In a medium bowl, mix flour, baking soda, and salt. Set aside. In a large bowl, cream butter and sugars. Beat in eggs and add vanilla. Mix the contents of the medium bowl into the contents of the large bowl. Stir in chips, and nuts if desired. Drop by teaspoonfuls, about 1 inch apart, onto ungreased cookie sheets. Bake at 375°F for 8 to 10 minutes, or until lightly browned. Cool completely. Makes about 4 dozen cookies.

• • • • • • • • • •

Eric Prater and his sons live in the beautiful Kittitas Valley on the eastern side of the Cascade Mountains, in Washington. They take pride in living in the home that Eric's great-grandfather built in 1915. In addition to farming, Eric works for the Ellensburg School District and the local farm cooperative. When he is not working, exploring, reading, or helping his sons with their homework, Eric can be found woodworking with antique tools.

"I love the outdoors—hiking, snowshoeing, and exploring the Cascades with my family and friends. Before going on an outdoor adventure, I make a batch of Ugly But Good Chocolate Chip Cookies to bring along (having already sampled a few when they're still warm). I like to bring along fresh cold milk to have with the cookies—obviously fairly early in the hike, before the milk gets warm. When camping overnight, one of our traditions is to make whole wheat griddlecakes for breakfast, served up hot with syrup, jam, or even whipped cream."

Cookies are great with ice cream. Try H. Adams Carter's Wind River Ice Cream, page 151.

Ralph Uber

Peak Peppernuts

2 cups sugar
2 cups dark corn syrup
1 cup butter or vegetable shortening
½ cup sour cream
1 teaspoon baking soda
11 cups flour (approximately; use enough to make a stiff dough)
1 teaspoon ginger
1 teaspoon allspice
1 teaspoon ground cloves
1 teaspoon ground nutmeg
2 teaspoons cinnamon
1 teaspoon salt
3 teaspoons baking powder
1 teaspoon crushed anise seeds
1 teaspoon cardamom seeds

Cream together the sugar, syrup, and shortening. Stir the soda into the sour cream, and add to the creamed mixture. Sift the flour, spices, salt, and baking powder together. Add anise and cardamom seeds. Mix the dry ingredients with the creamed mixture to form a stiff dough. Cut the dough into small pieces and roll into balls. Place balls on greased cookie sheets, and bake at 325°F for 15 minutes. Makes approximately 4 dozen.

• • • • • • • • • •

Ralph Uber, M.D., lives in Yakima, Washington, where he is a full-time alpaca and llama rancher, with more than 160 alpacas. After moving from Montana to Yakima in 1949, Ralph became interested in climbing. He has made many climbs in the Cascades. In the early 1960s, his various ascents included two new routes on the west side of Mount Adams. Ralph has also climbed in the Tetons, the Bugaboos, peaks in Oregon, a peak in Mexico, and the St. Elias Range in Alaska. As a licensed pilot, he has had exciting aviation adventures around the world.

"I once had a harrowing experience on Adams. I was climbing the icefall with Bob Swenson. The ice was exceptionally hard, and I was on a lead above Bob when I slipped. The only thing that saved me from severe injury or death was Bob's quick observation and action. He was able to jab his ice ax point a quarter-inch into the ice and hold me with his belay."

See peppernuts' lore on page 230.

Tempting Beverages

*H*ere is a sampling of favorite trail food beverages that seem to hit the mark, for either comforting warmth or thirst-quenching refreshment.

Coffee, chai, cider, a slush, a hot fruit drink, and the classic grog and Russian tea mixes are all included. And what about a great cup of cocoa to warm you up before you slide into your sleeping bag? Not only do they satisfy the taste buds, they also generate wonderful aromas.

In addition to the beverages offered in this chapter, take a look at Hans Fuhrer's Wild Herb Tea Mix, page 171, Gary McCue's recipe for Real Nepali Chiyaa (Chai), page 187, and Maynard Miller's recipe for Tibetan Tea, page 190.

Whatever "brew" you choose, it'll be great on the trail or in camp—all around the clock!

Tim Cahill

Fat Cocoa

1 packet of hot cocoa mix
6 to 8 ounces hot water
Sugar, to taste (optional)
1 to 2 tablespoons of butter

Dump cocoa mix into large cup. Add 6 ounces hot water (or amount directed on package). Stir in sugar and butter. Serves 1.

●　●　●　●　●　●　●　●　●　●

Tim Cahill writes for *National Geographic Adventure*, is an editor-at-large for *Outside* magazine, and is the author of nine books, including *Lost in My Own Backyard: A Walk in Yellowstone National Park* (Crown), *Hold the Enlightenment* (Vintage), and *Jaguars Ripped My Flesh* (Vintage). He grew up in Wisconsin, lives in Montana, and engages in winter camping, but is really a sissy about being cold.

"This drink, consumed just before sleep, puts some fat in the furnace and generally keeps burning all night long. I hate to sleep cold and I hate to wake up at 3 A.M. shivering and praying for the dawn. Also, it tastes good on a cold evening, and there is that pleasant aura of sin about eating fat for fat's sake."

June Fleming

Trail Coffee

June's Cowboy Coffee

For 6 servings, pour 6 cups of water into a pot. Add ½ cup ground coffee. When the brew comes to a full boil, remove the pot from the heat. Let it rest a few minutes, then tap the side of the pot to "settle" the grounds. For stronger coffee, add a bit more coffee before boiling.

Flavored Cowboy Coffee

Make this tasty rendition by adding a piece of hard candy to your hot java and stirring. Peppermint, chocolate mint, and amaretto coffee are delicious and aromatic.

June's Easy Trail Coffee

   1 cup instant coffee
   1 cup powdered nondairy creamer
   ¾ cup brown sugar
   1½ teaspoon pumpkin pie spice mix

At home, mix together ingredients. Store in a resealable plastic bag. At camp, for each serving, boil 1 cup water. Pour into a mug. Stir in 2 teaspoons of mix.

● ● ● ● ● ● ● ● ●

See June's recipes for Trail-Happy Salad, page 81, S'Mores Bars, page 150, and Protein Power Muffins, page 34. Her biography appears on page 34.

Jeff Renner

Trail Cider

1 quart apple cider
¼ orange (not peeled)
1 teaspoon whole cloves
¼ lemon (not peeled)
2 cinnamon sticks
1 cup orange juice
¼ cup lemon juice

On peel side, pierce orange with cloves. In a saucepan, combine cider, orange, lemon, and cinnamon sticks. Over medium heat, bring to boil. Boil gently for 5 minutes, then reduce heat and simmer for 10 more minutes. Add the orange and lemon juices. Let brew for a few minutes. Remove lemon and orange quarters. Keep hot in a thermos, to enjoy along the trail; or cool, then reheat in camp.

• • • • • • • • • •

"Core strength usually describes fitness; on a cold day, core strength can also mean keeping warm and energized. I've found this cider recipe is perfect for warming you up before diving into a sleeping bag on a chilly night. High places offer stunning views of the night sky. Being a bit of an amateur astronomer, I hate to turn in too early and miss the parade of celestial wonders, whether it's a meteor shower, the Milky Way, or the Northern Lights. Wrapping your hands around a mug of this cider keeps the chill at bay and the motivation strong to enjoy nature's night-time beauty."

See Jeff's recipe for Snow Cake, page 52. His biography appears on the same page.

Paul Richins

Sierra Slush

1 cup water
Powdered drink mix (Gatorade or your favorite)
Snow

Locate a snow bank and clear dirty snow from surface. Fill, but do not "pack," a 1-liter bottle with clean snow. Do not pack the snow into the water bottle, as there must be adequate empty space in the bottle for mixing the snow, water, and Gatorade. Add water and drink mix. Shake vigorously. Drink slowly and enjoy! Serves 1.

* * * * * * * * * *

"A tasty Sierra Slush is a refreshing beverage. Provided a snow bank is nearby, it is easy to make. However, be sure to drink it slowly. Too much of a good thing, too fast, can cause your esophagus, chest, lungs, and ribs to feel as though they are being frozen instantly."

See Paul's recipe for Mushroom Garlic Chicken Dinner, page 134, and Vegetable, Salmon, and Rice Dinner, page 122. His biography appears on page 122.

Bradford B. Van Diver

Russian Tea Mix

2 cups orange-flavored instant drink
4 scoops unsweetened lemonade-flavored drink mix
¾ cup unsweetened instant tea (plain or with lemon)
1 cup sugar
2 teaspoons cinnamon
1 teaspoon allspice
1 teaspoon ground cloves
Hot water

At home, combine dry ingredients. Transport mix in a resealable plastic bag. At camp, stir 2 teaspoons of tea mix into a cup of hot water.

• • • • • • • • • •

Bradford (Brad) Van Diver is professor emeritus in the College of Arts and Sciences at the State University of New York at Potsdam. He and his wife, Bev, reside in Black Mountain, North Carolina. In addition to hiking almost every week on the many trails near their home, they maintain a three-mile section of the Mountains-to-Sea Trail near the Blue Ridge Parkway. In recent years, Brad has climbed Grand Teton and Mount Assiniboine, in the Canadian Rockies. He teaches courses in creative retirement at the University of North Carolina in Ashville, Montreat College, and through Elderhostel. Brad is the author of *Roadside Geology of New York*, *Roadside Geology of Pennsylvania*, and *Roadside Geology of Vermont and New Hampshire* (all published by Mountain Press Publishing).

"A cup of Russian Tea should help get you to your summit. A couple of other camp beverages are good and easy to make. Stir 3 or 4 teaspoonfuls of fruit-flavored gelatin dessert into a cup of hot water (add orange-flavored instant drink or sweetened lemonade mix to taste). Or put equal parts of hot cocoa mix and instant coffee—each in normal amounts—into a cup of hot water."

Fred Stanley

Red-Hot Jell-O

3 to 4 tablespoons Jell-O (your favorite flavor)
10 ounces hot water

Place Jell-O in container with a tight-fitting lid. Pour in hot water. Place lid securely on container. Shake, then pour into a drinking cup. Be sure not to drink out of the container's lid, as Jell-O can "gum up" the threads of the lid.

• • • • • • • • • •

Fred Stanley and his wife, Dorothy, live in Ellensburg, Washington. He began climbing as a teenager, in 1961. Through the years he has been fortunate to have many climbers as mentors, rope mates, and friends. Fred has worked as a guide on Mount Rainier and elsewhere. He was a member of the American Alpine Club–sponsored 1974 American Pamirs/ U.S.S.R. Expedition. The following year, he was on the 1975 American K2 Expedition. Two popular Washington climbs in which Fred participated include the first ascents of the Liberty Crack Route on the East Face of Liberty Bell and the Burgner-Stanley Route on the South Face of Prusik Peak. He still enjoys the Cascades rock, snow, and ice; the Leavenworth granite; the Peshastin sandstone; the Vantage basalt; and the Tieton andesite. Currently Fred is a systems analyst for the Department of Computer Science, at Central Washington University. Dorothy's pound cakes are legendary among Fred's climbing companions, while his culinary skills are limited to toasting bread and boiling water.

"The Jell-O beverage is one of my favorites (especially the raspberry flavor) on a cold day. However, I have experienced other beverages that may appeal to those with more 'sophisticated' palates. One is Kirghiz Kumiss. Kumiss is fermented mare's or camel's milk. We were introduced to the following version by Kirghiz herdsmen in the Achik Tash Valley beneath Pik Lenin: Into a horsehide container, milk one sweaty mare that has been rolling in manure in her corral. Ferment at room temperature, uncovered to gather unidentified floating objects, until it smells like the sweaty mare. On festive occasions, pour into a communal drinking bowl and serve to visiting climbers too polite and too foolish to decline."

William N. Prater

Sherpa Grog

2 parts hot cocoa mix
2 parts dry milk
1 part sugar
Miniature marshmallows (optional)

At home, combine cocoa mix, dry milk, and sugar; add marshmallows if desired. Transport mix in a resealable plastic bag. At camp, measure about ⅓ cup of mix into a cup, and fill to brim with boiling water. Stir.

● ● ● ● ● ● ● ● ● ●

William (Bill) Prater, who lives in Cle Elum, Washington, has been an active mountaineer since 1949. He has made numerous climbs in the Cascades, including the first winter ascent of Mount Stuart. He has also climbed in the Rockies and in the Presidential Range of New Hampshire. In 1965 he was on the first ascent of 13,905-foot Mount Kennedy in the St. Elias Range in Yukon Territory, and in 1976 he climbed 20,320-foot Mount McKinley.

Bill was the first commercial manufacturer of lightweight snowshoes especially designed for mountain use. He had had much personal experience in floundering around on Pacific Northwest peaks on heavy, unwieldy wooden snowshoes with poor bindings. Thus inspired, he began to manufacture radically different snowshoes that included lightweight metal frames, traction devices, and a new type of binding that would accommodate any boot. His snowshoes caused a revolution in winter climbing in the areas for which they had been adapted and also proved practical for widespread recreational use.

"We began our own snowshoe manufacturing firm in 1971. At first we made bindings, traction kits, and ice ax baskets. In 1973 we started making aluminum-frame snowshoes in three models, and we added more models later. Our snowshoes were soon in use on major mountain expeditions from McKinley to the Antarctic, on K2, and to over 21,500 feet on Everest. We sold the controlling interest in our company in 1977, but I am still a consultant to the firm, designing and testing snowshoes and other new products that may be marketable in the future.

"I devised Sherpa Grog on winter snowshoe outings in the Stuart Range of the Cascades. It works well as part of an eating 'system' that requires only a way

to heat water, a cup, and spoon. At breakfast, mix the cereal in a cup, follow it with cocoa, and swab out the cup with snow. For dinner, start with soup in the cup; follow this with a mixture of instant potato, cheese, corned beef, lots of butter, and seasonings; end up with a cup of Sherpa Grog. Again clean out the cup with snow or water, and it's ready for the next meal. It's a good way to cut down on camp chores."

Read grog's lore on page 226.

Wild Food Feasting

A minimal knowledge of which wild foods are edible, which are really good, and which include deadly poison can be very useful information in case it becomes necessary to "live off the land." However, with the exception of fish and game (if there is enough to subsist on), wild foods are largely for fun and frills in most recreational outdoor pursuits.

Edible plants may range from peculiar to delicious. Their availability varies with region and season. However, at any time—particularly when supplies are scarce—judgment and restraint should be used when harvesting wild plants. Some species reproduce slowly; others have a hard time existing at all under adverse conditions, and even those that are abundant should be left in plentiful supply to give pleasure to others.

Books on the subject of edible plants include *Edible Wild Plants: A Pocket Guide* by Alan M. Cvancara (Ragged Mountain Press), *Edible and Medicinal Plants of the Rockies* by Linda Kershaw (Lone Pine Publishing), and *Harvesting Nature's Bounty: a Guidebook of Nature Lore, Wild Edible, Medicinal, and Utilitarian Plants and Animals* (e-book found at *Amazon.com*).

Most varmints, perhaps, are less subject to elimination than plants. They are usually difficult to capture and frequently seem to lack taste appeal (though they can be palatable). There may be some that are protected locally or are "off limits" for some reason. And of course, with nonvarmint game, and with fish, local laws must be observed.

Doug Benoliel

Cooked Stinging Nettles

2 to 3 cups boiling water
¼ to ½ cup fresh chopped onion
1 pinch sea salt
3 cups chopped stinging nettles (*Urtica dioica*)*
Butter
Fresh lemon or lime juice, or vinegar
Sea salt and black pepper, or lemon pepper and salt, to taste

*Wearing leather or heavy rubber gloves is advisable while gathering and chopping stinging nettles.

Bring 2 or 3 cups water to boil. Put in the chopped onion and sea salt. Add the chopped nettles (for best results, pick only the top 4 to 6 inches of young spring nettles). Boil the greens till they no longer have their stinging quality, about 5 minutes. Drain off liquid. Serve the hot nettles and onions topped with butter, several drops of lemon or lime juice or vinegar, sea salt, and other seasonings. This amount provides 2 servings of greens to accompany an evening meal.

● ● ● ● ● ● ● ● ● ●

Doug Benoliel of Kirkland, Washington, is a backpacker, botanist, landscape gardener, and contractor. His firm specializes in working with native plants. In the early 1970s he was an instructor at the National Outdoor Leadership School (NOLS). His book, *Northwest Foraging* (Signpost Books), arose from these varied interests.

"When hiking, I like to carry nine to twelve different spices and herbs—the longer the trip, the greater the variety desirable. A good dish using a wild mountain food as the principal ingredient is a hearty soup made from the leaves and stems of spring beauty (Claytonia lanceolata). By taking only one leaf or stem from each plant, no plant is destroyed. To make the soup, put a package of chicken noodle soup mix in a quart of boiling water. Add ¼ cup chopped onion; 1 tablespoon butter; 2 to 3 cups spring beauty leaves and stems; a pinch each of basil, black pepper, lemon pepper, dried watercress, and oregano; and 2 pinches each of garlic salt, celery salt, and sea salt. Simmer for 10 minutes before serving."

Eugenia Horstman Connally

Tasty Wild Plants

Many wild plants make tasty eating. Milkweed pods or buds are good. Choose tightly packed, green flower buds, or pods no longer than 1½ inches. Put them in a pot and pour boiling water over them. Boil 1 minute and drain. Repeat a couple of times. Cover the buds or pods with fresh boiling water, and boil for 10 minutes. Season with butter, salt, and pepper. All parts of the naturalized day lily (*Hemerocallis fulva*) are edible. Early spring sprouts are especially good; the inside white part is very tender and can be eaten raw, sliced into salads, or cooked. The green flower buds can be gathered when nearly ready to open, and boiled briefly. The underground tubers, if firm, are good either raw or boiled for 15 minutes. Or, to make Day Lily Soup, sauté 2 cups chopped tubers and spring shoots together with 8 small wild onions (chopped) in butter till tender. Add them to bouillon.

• • • • • • • • • •

Eugenia ("GG") Horstman Connally of Washington, D.C., is a former editor of *National Parks* magazine, a job in which she was able to combine her interests in art, literature, wildlife, and the outdoors.

"My favorite tramping ground is Shenandoah National Park in the Blue Ridge Mountains of Virginia—two hours' drive from Washington, D. C. I belong to a group of friends who assemble once a month at someone's home for a wild potluck dinner; at least one ingredient of each dish must be wild. During spring and summer we often go on camping trips where we forage for our dinner. Sometimes we go to a farm whose owner wants us to identify the wild foods growing on his property. In autumn we usually make a trip to Assateague Island National Seashore, which parallels the coast of Maryland and part of Virginia. There we sample crabs, clams, mussels, and oysters. One summer we went on a canoe 'survival' trip on the Shenandoah River with Joe Sottosanti, who runs a river outfitting concern near Luray, Virginia, and who for eight years fed his wife and four children entirely off the land and the river."

Hans Fuhrer

Wild Herb Tea Mix

Hips (fruits) of wild roses (*Rosa* species)
Berries of juniper (*Juniperus communis*)
Yarrow (*Achillea millefolium*)
Wild bergamot (beebalm, horsemint) (*Monarda fistulosa* var.
   menthaefolia)
Pineapple weed (*Matricaria matricarioides*)

To make the mix, first collect the herbs and berries during summer and fall. Dry slowly. The rose hips and juniper berries should be squashed before drying. The yarrow leaves and juniper berries are dominant in flavor and should be used in lesser quantities than the other herbs. Store mix in a resealable plastic bag. At camp, pour boiling water over a portion of the mixed herbs, and steep for 5 to 10 minutes. The brew has an excellent taste. Try it and you will like it.

* * * * * * * * * *

Hans Fuhrer of Radium Hot Springs, British Columbia, was born in Switzerland and immigrated to Canada in 1963. He is a full-time warden with the Canadian National Park Service and serves on the mountain rescue team.

"After a long, strenuous climb or hike, mountain food—no matter how it is prepared—always tastes better to us than the most expensive meal in a luxurious restaurant. There is the feeling that we have earned our food and that the occasion is special. In the wilderness we may be above timberline, on glaciers or high peaks, perhaps with days remaining before we reach our objective. There is always the possibility of atmospheric conditions changing for better or worse. We can survive only if, before a trip, we carefully prepare our equipment and food.

"My favorite breakfast during a leisure hike, when I can spend more time cooking, is a Cheese Crust Sandwich. Cut slices of cheese (any type). Put cheese into a frying pan over low heat, and let it melt slowly to a fine soft crust. Take the cheese crust out of the pan, and let it cool. Soak up cheese fat in the pan with bread, and brown bread gently. Place the cheese crust between the browned bread slices. For the final touch, fry some bacon or ham and combine with the Cheese Crust Sandwich. This can be washed down with coffee or Wild Herb Tea. Good!"

Ben Guild

Boiled Fiddlehead Ferns

Young curled fern heads of bracken fern (*Pteridium aquilinum*)
Salt and pepper
Butter or margarine

Pick the young tender "fiddlehead" fern shoots when they are 1 to 6 inches high. They are at their best when still shaped like fiddleheads. Wash, and remove the brown leaf covering. Boil until tender (½ to 1 hour) and season with salt, pepper, and butter. This makes a good vegetable dish to go with other camp foods. The young fern heads can also be fried in butter or margarine and eaten with toast or crackers. Or they can be eaten raw with salt.

• • • • • • • • •

Ben Guild of Eagle River, Alaska, is a naturalist. He has written many magazine articles about his experiences in recent years with wild foods and animals. He is the author of *The Alaska Mushroom Hunter's Guide* (Alaska Northwest Publishing), the definitive text of Alaskan fungi, and two other books: *The Alaska Psychoactive Mushroom Handbook* and *Home Grown Mushrooms in Alaska (or Anywhere Else) and How to Cook Them* (both published by Alaska Nature Press).

"I am preparing a new field guide dealing with the use of wild foods for outdoors people in Alaska. It will cover plants, leaves, roots, fruits, berries, and mushrooms, all common to Alaska. I spend five or six months a year in the

Alaska bush. By using wild foods, including game, I can cut my camp food bills in half and get into pretty good shape doing it.

"In 1973 I made the second major exploration in forty-three years of the great Aniakchak Caldera on the Alaska Peninsula. This extremely wild, remote volcanic area is a 'wilderness world within a mountain.' I spent six weeks by myself down inside the 6-mile-diameter, 3000-foot-deep caldera. Despite some raging storms with winds of hurricane velocity, I managed to photograph and document this amazing ecological phenomenon. I returned in 1976 and 1977 with a partner and reinforced my data on the area. During a six-week period in 1976–1977, we had an exclusive photographic exhibition on the Aniakchak Caldera at the National Park Service's regional headquarters in Anchorage. I worked closely with the National Park Service after the Aniakchak area was proposed as a new wilderness national monument. This has now been accomplished. The area is called the Aniakchak Wilderness National Monument. I hope in future years to be taking parties into this wilderness region."

Steve Markoskie

Oregon Grape Syrup

Ripe berries of Oregon grape (*Mahonia*)
Water
Sugar or honey, to taste

Combine ingredients. You only need a little water to make syrup with ripe berries. Boil for an hour or so, till of a syrupy consistency. This makes a very tasty pancake syrup. Try this syrup on the French toast, hotcakes, and pancakes found in "Daybreak Breakfasts," beginning on page 17.

. . . .

Steve Markoskie of Chehalis, Washington, was formerly an instructor at a United States Air Force survival school. He also taught outdoor recreation courses at Gonzaga University in Spokane and at Spokane Falls Community College. His classes included wilderness survival, first aid, backpacking, snowshoeing, and river rafting. Steve has climbed and snowshoed in the Rockies, Tetons, and Cascades.

"Knowing which wild plants are edible and which are poisonous is a pragmatic approach to outdoor understanding and enjoyment. Know the plants you eat. Do not eat unidentified beans, bulbs, fungi (mushrooms), or plants with milky sap or fine hairs. White berries generally contain a poison, while blue or black berries are usually safe to eat. But red berries can be either edible or poisonous depending on the variety, so specific berry knowledge is required.

"Several general tips about plant selection can be used to ensure the gatherer the best plants available under the most favorable conditions. Usually springtime or early summer provide the most abundant variety of wild foods. If possible look for plants in cool, shaded, moist areas. Immature plants taste less bitter and are more tender than mature ones—look for small shoots or buds that break crisply.

"Recipes can be complex or simple depending on several variables, but my favorites are generally quick and easy. First gather the plants and clean them thoroughly. Cook the wild food just as you do food at home, according to individual tastes. There is no great mystery. Boiling, baking, or steaming are my preferred methods.

"Wild foods provide a tasty and nutritious change in an often boring trail menu, and they don't have to be carried. They also can sustain a knowledgeable

outdoorsman under most 'normal' and emergency conditions. During one phase of Air Force survival training, our group walked a hundred miles cross-country, living off the land as much as possible. Another instructor and I stoned a grouse. The bird's crop was filled with just-eaten huckleberries. So in true survival fashion we all ate some. A few eyebrows were lifted, but this 'food experience' graphically illustrated more complete 'survival usage.'"

Larry Dean Olsen

Mouse Soup

Mouse (or other small rodent, as available)
Wild vegetables
Water

Skin and gut the mouse; be careful not to get the blood on your hands (this part isn't easy). Have water nearby to rinse with. Put the mouse in the sun to dry. While it is drying, boil wild vegetables in water. When the mouse meat is half dry, pulverize it, bones and all, to hamburger. Use the Indian grinding method of pounding the meat on a concave or flat rock (a *metate*) with a smaller handheld rock (a *mano*). When the mouse is pulverized, add it to the boiling vegetables. The meat should be done in about 10 minutes. You can substitute packrat, woodrat, desert kangaroo rat, woodchuck (lowland marmot), ground squirrel, etc., for the mouse.

● ● ● ● ● ● ● ● ● ●

Larry Dean Olsen is the author of *Outdoor Survival Skills* (Chicago Review Press). For many years, with a trained staff, he taught survival techniques in Montana, Utah, and Nevada. In 1988, Larry began Wilderness Conquest, now called Wilderness Quest. He is also a founding member of the National Association of Therapeutic Wilderness Camps and the ANASAZI Foundation, a nonprofit wilderness treatment program for troubled teens and their parents.

"I learned survival methods on my own when I was growing up around Jerome in southern Idaho. I started teaching professionally in the mid-1960s. Students in such courses often arrive with absolutely no survival knowledge. They learn to live off the land without any utensils or previously manufactured items—with only their bare hands in the desert/alpine environment of the western United States. But living off the land is pretty much the same worldwide: you learn to use what is there.

"Among the edible plants found all over the arid West is biscuitroot (Cogswellia or Lomatium *species), which belongs to the carrot family; it is also called cous or cowish. The Lewis and Clark Expedition called it 'Bread of Cows' and traded horses to get it for food.*

"Cattail roots make good flour. Carry this or flour from home in a pouch. To make Ash Cakes, scoop a little hole in the flour with your fingers, and pour enough water into the pouch to make part of the flour into dough. Pinch off

pieces about the size of golf balls; with your hands, form cakes shaped like tortillas. Drop into hot campfire coals. Turn once. Roast cakes for about 5 minutes, pull them out, cool, and blow off ashes. Spread with butter and jam (if any), and eat. Wild berries can be sealed inside the folded cake before cooking.

"Wild plants are generally socially acceptable, but lots of people get squeamish about eating small rodents. However, those who can't stand to see mice and rats being cooked can enjoy the flavor. Mouse meat tastes remarkably good— something like beef."

Barry Prather

Juneau Icefield Go-Atter Stew

1 spotted go-atter
4 glugs water
Dash salt and pepper
1 carrot (fresh or dried)
1 onion (fresh or dried)
Dehydrated potatoes, to taste

A go-atter is a bushy-tailed packrat or woodrat. (Woodrats are distinguished from house rats by hairy-not-scaly tails. Bushy-tailed woodrats have squirrel-like tails and usually live above the pine belt. The Juneau Icefield go-atter is *Neotoma cinerea*.) After catching and cleaning the go-atter, put 4 glugs of water in the pot—a glug is the sound water makes when poured from a plastic canteen tipped at a 45-degree angle. Bring water to a boil. Add seasonings, vegetables, and go-atter. Boil till the smell drives you out of your tent or snow cave. Then you are ready to eat anything else. Recommended when regular climbing food becomes unpalatable (or scarce). Four field mice can be substituted for 1 go-atter. Note: The preparer might not want to clean the go-atter before using— probably save on seasoning.

. . . .

The late Barry Prather of Ellensburg, Washington, was a geophysicist whose work has included a fifty-three-day stint on top of 14,410-foot Mount Rainier, twenty summers on the Juneau Icefield in Alaska, three trips to the polar ice north of Alaska, and an austral summer in Antarctica. He was also a climber and a member of the 1963 Mount Everest Expedition. Tragically, in September 1987, Barry and his teenage son, Eric, died in an automobile accident.

"In 1959, when taking part in a project that was seeking a high-elevation site to test astronauts, I planted pinto beans on the side of a steam fumarole on top of Mount Rainier—it was probably the highest garden ever planted in the contiguous forty-eight states. The seeds germinated in only a week; but when the sprouts were an inch and a half tall, the air temperature frosted them. We tried hot caps over the plants, but the warm vapor steamed them to death.

"On the Everest expedition, I assisted Dr. Maynard Miller in geologic research. Subsequently I became an assistant of Dr. Miller's in research on the Juneau Icefield. One year we made the unusual discovery that woodrats were living in

a nearby nunatak—they didn't turn out to be our favorite form of wildlife. In 1976–1977 I was in Antarctica for the National Science Foundation. The Ross Ice Shelf is 30,000 square miles of perfectly flat terrain, with a continual wind mostly from the south in the austral summer and from the north in winter.

"One climbing meal I will never forget is a macaroni-and-cheese dinner I was boiling up in a snow cave. Just as it was ready to eat, I tipped over the stove, the pot flew, and the food spilled out all over our snow bed. I grabbed a nearby shovel, scooped up the mess—and it was quickly eaten, pine needles and all. But thereafter I was relieved of all cooking chores."

Rainer Brocke

Baked Squirrel In Foil

1 squirrel
Bacon strips

Completely skin and clean squirrel. Cut body of squirrel into 2 portions. Wrap meat with strips of bacon. Wrap meat and bacon in foil; crimp the edges of the foil carefully. Cook until the meat falls off the bones. This should be done in an oven or over a bed of coals, but with care could also be done in a covered pan over a one-burner stove. Game birds such as grouse or pheasant cooked the same way generally turn out rather well. Skin and clean the bird, but leave it whole for cooking. Meat prepared by this method goes well with potatoes and a vegetable of one's choice. This recipe serves 1 (but 2 squirrels per person might be required).

• • • • • • • • • •

Rainer Brocke of Lafayette, New York, is professor emeritus of Wildlife Ecology at the College of Environmental Science and Forestry in the State University of New York at Syracuse. He has long been an enthusiastic backpacker and hunter.

"Years ago we used to live on a farm. Each fall I had the opportunity to hunt fox squirrels there; they were quite abundant. When I discovered this recipe, our whole family—including my daughter, who was then three years old—became 'nutty' about squirrels cooked this way. This dish was often served to guests of ours, particularly those who turned up their noses at game. Their expressions of delight had to be seen to be believed. There is a nutlike taste to squirrel meat that is somehow complemented by the smoky flavor of bacon. Also, the bacon fat bastes the meat—game is usually dry—and the foil keeps in the moisture. Two squirrels per person are usually sufficient. The recipe is not original with me, but I have used it many times and can vouch for it. For backpackers and hunters it is tremendous. Rabbit or grouse can be substituted for squirrel.

"This recipe is deceptively simple, considering the fantastic results! The end result is hard to match with the most elaborate cuisine."

Sandy Bryson

Halfmoon High Trout

White flour
Salt, pepper, and *herbs garni*, to taste
Trout
½ cup olive oil
Almonds, finely chopped
Wild herbs (onion, bay leaves, coriander, watercress, etc.)
    if available
Chardonnay or sauterne
Wild greens (optional side dish)

At home, mix flour, salt, pepper, and *herbs garni*. Seal well in a resealable plastic bag. At camp, catch and clean trout. Shake fish in the flour bag. Sauté in a pan with olive oil, almonds, any available wild herbs, and wine. (If the trout outsmart you, substitute freeze-dried chicken.) Serve with wild salad greens such as watercress or wild lettuce, if there are any.

● ● ● ● ● ● ● ● ● ●

Sandy Bryson of Alpine County, California, has been a police and rescue dog handler and trainer since 1974. She instructs police dog teams for law enforcement agencies and has participated in numerous rescue missions, taught avalanche rescue techniques, been a Forest Service wilderness ranger, and been a member of a canine ranger team in Yosemite National Park. Sandy founded the first rescue dog unit in California. She is the author of *Police Dog Tactics* (Detselig Enterprises) and *The Vancouver Island Traveler* (Windham Bay Press).

"We spend so much time backpacking that the food we carry is as important as warm clothing and shelter. In recent years, the quality of freeze-dried food has improved markedly, and on rescue missions I eat a lot of it—plus other space-age material such as gorp, candy, and fast foods. But when skiing or hiking for fun, I prefer to sacrifice light weight for culinary regalement.

"A delicious nonwild camp dish is stuffed potatoes. At home, bake 2 to 4 potatoes until skins begin to turn crisp and the insides are tender. Slit skin, and hollow out potatoes without puncturing the casing. Mix potato meat with 1½ cups shredded cooked chicken, 1 cup grated sharp cheddar cheese, 1 cup chopped shallots, salt, pepper, and ½ cup white wine; stuff back into potato skins, and wrap individually in heavy foil for reheating in campfire embers or over a

stove. These stuffed potatoes keep indefinitely on cold-weather trips, and for a day or two in warm weather (chill or freeze them before a trip).

"My funniest food experience was on a search where my dog found a lost twelve-year-old girl who had done all the right things to keep from freezing to death overnight. She was hungry after her ordeal. Another handler and I dug into our packs for food. When my partner offered her gorp laced with chocolate candies, she very solemnly refused it. She proceeded to wolf down all my dried apricots and jerky, commenting, 'Candy is bad for you. I really never touch the stuff!'"

Charlie Norton

Deep-Fried Trout Crispies

Small trout, such as midnight blues or square-tails
Lard or other fat, a soup-can full for deep frying

Eastern trout are different from those in the West. They aren't very big, only 3 or 4 inches long, almost minnow-size. (Consult the local game laws!) Capture a lot of them. As you catch them, fry them on the spot in deep fat. Don't clean them—the deep frying crisps them. Eat the entire fish—head, tail, everything. Excellent!

* * * * * * * * * *

Charlie Norton of Saratoga Springs, New York, has skied, snowshoed, and backpacked for over twenty-five years. He is a gunsmith by trade, specializing in muzzle loaders.

"My favorite area is here in the Adirondacks. This is great backcountry for hiking, skiing, and snowshoeing. Many people who have only read about New York think of the entire state in terms of New York City. They don't realize that we have a lot of wooded, hilly, rural terrain. Adirondack State Park is big, larger than some of our neighboring states, and is a very beautiful area. I enjoy the nearby mountains year-round.

"I have some good recipes to use when a campfire is possible. One is for pike. Catch one big enough to clean with an axe, and chop out about 5 pounds. Don't scale it. In summer, stuff the chunk of fish with wild onions and dandelion greens (add butter or other fat because it is a dry fish), or stuff it with an onion dressing. Wrap fish in aluminum foil, and roast it over campfire coals. Allow about 20 minutes per side; turn once. Pull the bundle out of the coals, unwrap, and it should be done.

"A good way to cook a duck, if you can get one, is to roast it in clay. Collect a good-sized mound of blue clay from along a river or lake. Clean (but do not remove feathers from) the duck, remove its insides, and fill the cavity with leftover corn bread and an onion stuffing mix. Mound clay over the duck on the ground, working the clay into the feathers until it is well covered. Build a fire on the mound to get a good bed of hot coals. Let the coals burn for some 6 hours. Pull off the coals, and split open the clay mound with an axe. The duck's feathers and skin peel off, and the meat and stuffing remain. Delicious eating."

Stephen C. Porter

Boiled Tuktu

Tuktu (caribou) ribs or thighs
Water to cover
Salt
Mayonnaise (optional)

Cover caribou ribs or thighs with water to cover and boil till tender. This is how the Nunamiut Eskimos of northern Alaska cook caribou. It tastes best with plenty of salt, or even better with mayonnaise.

• • • • • • • • • •

Stephen C. Porter is professor emeritus of Earth and Space Sciences at the University of Washington in Seattle. He has carried out glacial-geologic research in many of the world's most rugged and remote mountain ranges, and for twenty years has studied the monsoon climate history of central China and the Tibetan Plateau. For twenty-five years he was editor of the international journal *Quaternary Research*.

"I have been going into the mountains for more than thirty years, for both climbing and research. In recent years, my travels have been mostly in connection with various research projects involving the glacial history of high mountain areas. These include such places as the Brooks Range in Alaska, the Cascade Range of the Pacific Northwest, the Chilean Andes, the Italian Alps, the Hindu Kush in central Asia, the Himalaya, the mountains of Antarctica, the Southern Alps of New Zealand, and Hawaiian volcanoes.

"My work has, of course, often involved me in local recipes and ingredients. Boiled caribou was one of my favorite meat dishes in the central Brooks Range during four summers spent in northern Alaska. Roast caribou is good—but for a tasty change, try boiling it.

"Not long ago I was working on the recent glacial history of the southern flank of the Mont Blanc (Monte Bianco) massif in Italy. There the local food and wine were so good that I didn't have to resort to trail cooking."

Ethnic Adaptations

*T*hese trail food options speak for themselves.

Our well-traveled outdoor adventurers share ethnic discoveries they've made, adding a few twists of their own. The adventurer in each of us, by trying these recipies, can experience a variety of cultures through these culinary offerings.

Be sure to take the time to read their stories, too. You'll think you were right there, in another part of the world.

Gary McCue

Real Nepali Chiyaa (Chai)

¼ teaspoon cinnamon powder
⅛ teaspoon cardamom powder, or 4 crushed cardamom seeds
1 to 2 pinches of clove powder, or 4 crushed cloves
2 to 4 tablespoons sugar, or honey, to taste*
½ to ¾ cup milk powder, to taste
4 cups water, or 2 cups water combined with 2 cups whole milk
1 small handful tea leaves, or contents from 4 tea bags

*Traditionally, honey is not used as a sweetener in South Asian tea.

At home, mix together cinnamon, cardamom, and clove powders. Place in a resealable plastic bag. At camp, mix powdered milk with 1 cup water in a container. In a saucepan, bring 3 cups water (or combination of 1 cup water and 2 cups whole milk) to boil. Add powdered milk mixture to boiling water. Stirring constantly, add spices and sugar (or honey). Return to boil. Add tea and continue to stir. Return to boil for about 1 minute. Remove from the heat. Cover, and let stand for 5 minutes. Usually the tea leaves sink to the bottom, making a tea strainer unnecessary. Serves 4.

• • • • • • • • • •

See Gary's s recipe for Superfast Jumbo Jet All Morning Organic Porridge, page 26. His biography appears on the same page.

Mike Cheney and Purma Topgay Sherpa

Sherpa Soup

1 liter water
100 grams *sommer* (Sherpa cheese)
Garlic, to taste
Some chili
Tomato sauce, small amount

To boiled water, add *sommer,* garlic, chili, and tomato sauce. Boil for 5 minutes. Serves 4. "It is very good for climbing," says the Sherpa cook, "because it makes good feeling for the climbers."

Shyakpa

Vegetable oil
¼ kilogram onion
½ kilogram meat
1 kilogram potatoes
1 big spoon flour
Butter
1 liter water
Chili, small amount

Put some salad oil in a frying pan. As soon as it gets hot, add chopped onion. When the onions are browned, add meat. Add potatoes, and cook covered for 30 minutes. While meat, onion, and potatoes are cooking, make flour gravy. Melt butter in a pan, and add flour. Cook mixture till it gets brown; stir as necessary. Add water and chili, and boil for 6 minutes, Add this gravy to the meat and potatoes. Serves 4.

• • • • • • • • • •

The late Mike Cheney was British and lived in Kathmandu, Nepal, where he had more than twenty years of trekking experience. He was executive director of a trekking service of which Dawa Norbu Sherpa was the founder and chief executive.

"Our trekking outfit, with headquarters in Kathmandu, is the only cooperative organization in tourism in Nepal that strives for grassroots involvement of local people in the economic development of their region. We offer tailor-made treks for individuals and groups to all the major trekking areas of Nepal, and

also to many regions that are hardly on the trekking map. We played a leading role in the 1975 British expedition that put up the new and difficult Southwest Face Route on Everest. We were also organizing agents for the 1976 American Bicentennial Everest Expedition and other major expeditions.

"These recipes were provided by Purma Topgay Sherpa (now deceased), who was head cook for the 1975 British Everest Expedition and was on the staff of our trekking agency. Some of the ingredients are strictly local, necessitating substitutions if the dishes are prepared in other areas."

Maynard Miller

Tibetan Tea

4 or 5 cups water
1 or 2 tablespoons Darjeeling tea
½ teaspoon salt (or less, to taste)
1 tablespoon butter
Sugar, to taste (optional)

Bring water to boil. Add tea, and steep for 15 minutes without boiling again. Add salt and butter. Add sugar if desired. (Tibetans do not use sugar in tea.) Drink immediately, or carry in vacuum bottle. Shake well before drinking. It is a good trail tea, as the salt is beneficial and the butter provides a lift. Darjeeling is an Indian tea grown in the Himalayan foothills in southeastern Nepal.

● ● ● ● ● ● ● ● ● ●

Dr. Maynard Miller is professor of geology and dean of the College of Mines and Earth Resources at the University of Idaho in Moscow. He has served as director of Idaho's State Geological Survey, and is director of the Foundation for Glacier and Environmental Research. A geologist by profession, Dr. Miller has led or participated in more than seventy research and exploration projects in more than eighty countries. Among them is the first American ascent of Mount St. Elias in Alaska (1946). He was field leader on the Mount Kennedy and Mount Hubbard Memorial Mapping Yukon Expedition (1965).

"My two favorite locations in the world are similar. They have challenging and invigorating climates. One is the Alaska Yukon–British Columbia border region, which extends from the coast of Alaska through temperate rain forests in the Coast Mountains, on inland across the continental flank of the Boundary Range. September is the most memorable month of the year in the interior: Indian summer, flies and mosquitoes are gone, and the aspens are gold. The second region I particularly like is the Fitzroy area in Patagonia. It is very similar to the first; but in the southern hemisphere, autumn comes in March. Then instead of aspens turning gold, it's leaves of the Nothofagus tree in glowing crimson.

"In various places our expeditions have lived off the hinterland. In the Amazon you can eat Amazonian ants fried in oil as part of your meat supply. In Patagonia for months at a time we ate mutton, and occasionally shanks of skewered lamb, that were first barbecued in sunflower oil, and then eaten by hand with cooked

onions and potatoes. At every meal, in southern Patagonia and Chile, we drank maté with the natives. This is a mildly sedative native tea made from the yerba buena plant (Ilex paraguariensis) that grows in the jungles of Paraguay. The natives relax around the asado (barbecue) campfire passing a small gourd filled with hot maté. You sip it through a silver or brass straw known as a bombilla. If you don't imbibe when the bowl is passed, it is considered rude, verging on an insult."

Yvon Chouinard

Chimi Churi

1 small handful chopped garlic
½ cup vegetable oil
1 teaspoon red chili peppers
2 tablespoons salt
1 handful chopped green onions
Red wine vinegar
1 handful fresh oregano leaves

Combine ingredients. Put them in wine bottles, and top off with red wine vinegar. Make some vertical grooves in the corks so you can make shakers out of the bottles. Chimi Churi will keep for years, and you can keep adding more oil and vinegar as it runs out. It is delicious on meat cooked over a fire, especially wild game.

● ● ● ● ● ● ● ● ●

Yvon Chouinard is the founder and owner of Patagonia Inc. He designed and manufactured rock climbing equipment in the late 1950s. His tinkering led to an improved ice ax that is the basis for modern ice ax design. Yvon spends much of his time in the outdoors and serving on the boards of numerous environmental groups. He describes his job as that of the "outside" man, studying lifestyles around the world, coming up with ideas for new products, to assure that Patagonia stays relevant in a rapidly changing world. Since 1985, Patagonia Inc. has pledged one percent of sales to the preservation and restoration of the natural environment.

"Chimi Churi is especially recommended for Argentina and Patagonia. One use is with Lamb Carne Asada (barbecued lamb), prepared in this way:
  1. *Walk out of the mountains starving, to the nearest estancia (ranch). Make friends with the gauchos. Kill a lamb and leave skin on fence.*
  2. *Make fire and let it burn down to coals. Spear the whole lamb above the coals, and turn as necessary.*
  3. *Sprinkle with Chimi Churi, frequently.*
  4. *Cut off pieces of lamb as they get done. Smother in Chimi Churi, and eat with loud laughter, using your knife only.*

"Huevos Rancheros is a good dish anytime—in South America, Asia, Africa, Canada, or Yosemite. Make it this way:
  1. *Barter for 1 egg per person (cigarettes are excellent for barter, which also reduces your companions' supply). Stir up egg with salt and pepper.*

2. *Find a local vegetable (zucchini, eggplant, cabbage, tomato, wad of greens, etc.). Chop and sauté in fat with crushed garlic, onions, cheese, and mushrooms. (In the Orient, soak mushrooms overnight.)*
3. *While vegetables sauté, cut a hot pepper in half. Taste gingerly, and add to the vegetables, a tiny bit at a time until they are properly piquant but tolerable to the timid.*
4. *Heat more fat in separate skillet, pour in egg, and tilt skillet so egg will spread thin. Cook until jelled but not brown.*
5. *Flop egg onto plate, spoon in vegetables, and roll up to eat.*
6. *Repeat until egg and vegetable supplies are exhausted."*

John Roskelley

Himalayan Chapatis

Atta (whole pastry flour; in India, finely ground wheat flour
or meal)
Water
Strong hands, griddle, and hot coals

Add small quantities of water to an eyeballed amount of *atta,* depending on how many chapatis you want. Knead dough thoroughly with hands, and add water as needed to make dough similar in consistency to that of bread. Kneading is crucial and must be done thoroughly. Take a small gob of dough, and form it into a ball smaller than a tennis ball. With thumbs on top of the ball and index fingers underneath, rotate wad of dough to form a flat circular cake about the size of the average pancake but much thinner, similar to a crepe. Holding the cake between your hands in the clap position, start slapping it back and forth, rotating it as you slap it. The importance of having thin cakes, and their being well kneaded, cannot be overstressed.

Put the cake on a flat griddle that has been preheated on coals. Leave for 10 to 20 seconds, until large bubbles form and the outer layer begins to brown. Then flip it to the other side, and cook for another 10 to 20 seconds. When both sides are done, serve plain or with butter or jam. Plain is most likely, since you wouldn't be eating these if you had anything else.

• • • • • • • • • •

John Roskelley of Spokane, Washington, has climbed extensively in Nepal, Pakistan, India, and elsewhere for the past thirty-seven years. He is the author of three books on adventures in mountaineering, *Nanda Devi: The Tragic Expedition* (The Mountaineers Books), *Stories Off the Wall* (The Mountaineers Books), and *Last Days* (Stackpole Books). His photography has been on the cover of *National Geographic* as well as on the covers of numerous books, catalogs, and magazines. John is best known for his climbs up difficult and technical Himalayan routes, such as the West Pillar of 27,825-foot Makalu, the West Face of 23,440-foot Gaurisankar, the Northeast Face of 21,535-foot Tawoche, the Northwest Face of 25,645-foot Nanda Devi, and the East Face Direct of 20,000-foot Uli Biaho. He has climbed four 8000-meter peaks, including Dhaulagiri, K2, Makalu, and, most recently, at the age of fifty-four, Mount Everest via the North Col Route. John and his wife, Joyce, have been married for thirty-two years and have three great kids.

"I am no cook. Cheese and salami have been my mainstays. However, through too many of my travels in the East, I have had to survive on the local bread—variously known as chapatis, chaapatis, or chapattys. I have tried my hand at making these bread cakes, but with a certain lack of success. But in Nepal, Pakistan, and India every child from age three on can make them. So maybe American backpackers could too."

Great Food,
Less Work

*O*utdoor menus seem to become simpler and easier as hikes get harder, climbs longer, and the interest in photography, nature study, etc. greater. Apparently there are many ways of eating adequately without wasting much time on cooking.

Outdoorspeople who don't want to cook (but do have to eat) have developed many novel ways of surviving. A few outstanding personalities of the good old days did it by mooching: a talented young man with only a loaf of bread in his pack could gourmandize for days on samples from his friends' cookpots.

More widely applicable methods (that are also potentially less hazardous to the health) are described in this section. It must be noted that eating fairly well, while not cooking at all, may require more natural flair than just cooking.

George Schaller

Go With the Flow

"When on a project, I usually travel only with local people. They cook what they want, in the way they like, and I eat what they share with me; I don't carry special Western foods or ingredients. In the mountains of Laos, for example, the Hmong walk through the forest and pick up leaves, roots, land crabs, frogs, and other edible items and place them in a small basket. When we camp, they dump the contents of the basket into a pot and boil it into a sort of stew. It is no doubt nutritious, but I would not necessarily designate it as a favorite of mine. I also join local hosts in their tent, yurt, or hut for semi-outdoor meals that have included such items as rotten yak liver and boiled horse penis, though usually meals just consist of bland rice, manioc, noodles, and tsamba. Quite versatile, tsamba is made of roasted barley, ground into very fine flour, which is mixed with a little tea and then rolled into small lumps and eaten with fingers. It can also be made into soup, por-ridge, and other dishes. Most peoples seldom get meat. As a result, my mea-ger cooking skills have degenerated even further but my stomach has become exceptionally tolerant."

• • • • • • • • • •

George B. Schaller is a naturalist with the Wildlife Conservation Society in New York. He has spent most of his time in the wilds of Asia, Africa, and South America, and has studied species as diverse as the mountain gorilla, lion, jaguar, tiger, giant panda, and wild sheep and goats of the Himalaya. He has authored fifteen books, including *The Last Panda* (University of Chicago Press).

Colby Coombs

Haybros

"The favorite meal on a glacier with all the guides is a bit boring, but a huge hit—hash browns, or haybros. They are the best way to start the morning! For three hungry eaters or four not-so-hungry eaters, start with a pound of freeze-dried hash browns. Leave them in the bag you repackaged them in and fill with boiling water till they are covered. Seal off the bag. This method works well, or you can place the hash browns in a pot, add boiling water and cover with a lid. That dirties a pot, which is less efficient.

"While the haybros are rehydrating, warm up pre-cooked bacon in a deep frying pan. I have one made by Banks Fry Bake Company. Remove the bacon and put a BIG chunk of butter in the pan. When melted, add the haybros and spread them out evenly with a metal (not nylon) spatula. Turn the pan clockwise one-third revolution at a time, so that the entire bottom layer of potatoes gets crispy and golden brown. Add salt, pepper, Italian seasoning, and garlic powder. Slice enough cheese to cover the top. After 5 minutes, flip all the browns and add a layer of cheese to the top. Cover the pan with the lid. After 5 minutes, they are ready to serve with your choice of smoked salmon, salsa, hot sauce, more bacon, or nutritional brewer's yeast. Some people even like to add egg powder or scrambled egg mix. These are definitely not for the calorie or weight conscious.

"At 17,200 feet on Denali, on day four of a storm, sometimes the only thing climbers have to look forward to is the next meal. It is much easier to motivate people with haybros than an 'instant bloatmeal.'

"Haybros are so popular that the rations room at the school uses a 50-gallon garbage bin on wheels to store their supply. Next to coffee, hash browns are the most popular food item."

• • • • • • • • • •

Colby Coombs and his wife, Caitlin Palmer, of Talkeetna, Alaska, own and operate the Alaska Mountaineering School, where they share their knowledge and experience with students who learn to put safe travel techniques above "peak bagging." Colby summitted Denali in 1986, when he was eighteen years old. The following year he began instructing for the National Outdoor Leadership School (NOLS). He has written several books on climbing in Alaska, including *Denali's West Buttress—A Climber's Guide to McKinley's Classic Route* (The Mountaineers Books). In addition to climbing Denali many times, he has climbed in Wyoming, Colorado, Peru, and Alaska. The school's website is *www.climbalaska.org.*

Bill Sumner

Suharee

"Suharee can be made by drying any bread, including pan breads such as cornbread and chapatis. One delight is that any bread can be dried, including those found in exotic bazaars, with little danger of getting sick. Of all my favorite foods, suharee is most treasured because it keeps indefinitely, as long as it is kept dry, and I can eat with pleasure even when my stove has failed or when my stomach is rejecting yet another shrink-wrapped freeze-dried gut bomb. I eat Suharee by dipping it into a favorite soup or beverage, or even water, or simply gnaw on it when nothing else is available.

"My two favorite breads to dry are sourdough baguettes from our local Vinman's bakery and Uzbek laposhkee, marvelous round loaves of bread that are a bit like the result of marrying a wood-fired Frisbee with a donut. Both are indescribably delicious hot from the oven, but are hardly worse weeks later after being dried intact. Both carry well in a rucksack.

"During the Cold War, when Flura (who later became my wife) flew alone from Moscow to New York City, she was not sure if anyone would meet her. She carried a bag of Suharee, made the night before in a friend's oven from her favorite dense Baradinsky rye bread. With no money, and possibly no one to meet her at the airport, she was certain not to go hungry."

⦁ ⦁ ⦁ ⦁ ⦁ ⦁ ⦁ ⦁ ⦁

Bill Sumner is a physicist who lives near Ellensburg, Washington. He loves simple solutions to complex problems. Bill has climbed in mountain ranges around the world.

Lou Whittaker

Eat Like You Would at Home

"As a mountain guide, I always tell my climbers, 'If you want the mountains to feel like home you eat and drink what you would at home.'

"In the 1960s the trend for mountain climbing food included primarily proteins. It was always okay. Then the trend swung to climbers primarily consuming carbohydrates. I don't believe that carbohydrates are as efficient as protein, but everyone has a preference. My theory is that climbers should eat what they like at home and hydrate all along the way. Drinking lots of water and other liquids helps fend off mountain sickness. Drink as much as you can, and eat well and often. You don't have to limit yourself to three meals per day. Rather, eat a little bit all day long.

"One of my most vivid memories is of a climb on Kangchenjunga, the third highest peak in the world, located in eastern Nepal. I took along coffee, which I really like. When we ran out of it, I literally rifled through our garbage dump (that we built to pack out) to find old coffee grounds to brew again. That sounds a bit extreme, but it's what I had to do. The lesson learned: I need to take along plenty of coffee.

"On an added note, I cannot emphasize enough the importance of preserving the natural environment and the need to practice ecological courtesy. Don't bury trash; carry it out."

· · · · · · · · · ·

Lou Whittaker lives at the base of Mount Rainier's west side, in Ashford, Washington. He and his twin brother, Jim, climbed Mount Rainier for the first time at age sixteen. Lou led the first American ascent of Everest's north wall in 1984, and he led the first American summit of Kangchenjunga in 1989. He has summitted Mount Rainier more than 250 times and climbed in Alaska and the Karakoram. In 1968, Lou cofounded Rainier Mountaineering Inc. (RMI). Lou has instilled his priorities of mountain safety and guest experience in the alpine guide service. Under his guidance, RMI pioneered on-mountain instructional seminars that have become the standard for guide services across the country. In addition to Mount Rainier, RMI operates on Mount McKinley. In more than thirty-five years of operation, they have guided more than 65,000 climbers. Today, Lou's sons, Peter and Win, are also involved in the business. Lou is the author of *Lou Whittaker: Memoirs of a Mountain Guide* (The Mountaineers Books).

Dave Felkley

BIGfoot Wine and Cheese Snowshoe Tour

Wines (red and white)
Juice or sparkling cider (for those who prefer non-alcoholic beverages)
Cheeses (variety depends on tastes)
Breads, baguettes, cocktail loaves, or fancy crackers
Picnic tablecloth (red-and-white-checked is festive)
Plastic ants (to sprinkle on the tablecloth)
Sitting pads (foam squares)
Sled or backpacks
Snowshoes and poles
Snow!
Possible additions: Nuts, olives, pickles, carrots, celery, peppers, salami, pepperoni, and cookies

This is a BIGfoot special "recipe" for a good time on the white stuff of winter. There is no need to hibernate or develop cabin fever. Mix the above ingredients with a group of friends, family, or coworkers. Set a date and rent snowshoes and poles. Put together your own day tour, or call a guide service to arrange everything.

• • • • • • • • • •

Dave Felkley of Nederland, Colorado, is the editor of the fourth and fifth editions of Gene Prater's book, *Snowshoeing: From Novice to Master* (The Mountaineers Books). After many years in the corporate automotive world

with Nissan and Mercedes-Benz, Dave traded cars for snowshoes, wingtips for hiking boots, and freeways for mountain trails. While still licensed to drive, he hasn't owned a car for thirteen years and rides a scooter instead. Dave is semi-retired, and for nearly two decades he has operated BIGfoot Snowshoe Tours. For more information, visit *www.nederlandchamber.org.*

"Preparation for wine and cheese outings takes some time and is almost a party itself, if done by the group the day before. Prior to the tour, quiz the participants, then select the wines and cheeses. Be sure to go easy on the sampling, so that you'll have food and wine to take with you on the snowshoe tour!

"For large groups, select red and white wines in 1.5-liter bottles or 3-liter boxes. For smaller groups, standard 750-milliliter bottles provide more options. Have your local wine purveyor help you select wines within your budget. Remember, you and the guests will be carrying the wines on your backs, or pulling them on a sled.

"When selecting cheeses, keep in mind guest preferences—and the budget. There are great cheeses available that taste great and add sophistication. From jug wine with Velveeta to vintage wines with Roquefort or Brie, the fun factor is up to the group and the imagination of the host. If someone doesn't have fun, it is probably his or her own fault!

"Just a reminder—don't forget the details, such as a corkscrew, plastic wineglasses, knife and cutting board, and napkins. Some cheeses may require plastic knives and forks. In cases of extreme laziness, the group can always arrange for a pizza delivery at the parking lot, after returning from the snowshoe tour."

Peter Lev and Rod Newcomb

Mono-menus

"The idea that you have to take certain foods to eat while climbing is baloney. On McKinley we had the same food for breakfast, lunch, and dinner for fifty consecutive days. For breakfast we had hot whole wheat cereal with milk and sugar. Lunch was invariably green pea soup mix. Dinner was always macaroni and cheese or spaghetti, with two cups of hot chocolate. The only food we didn't get tired of eating after fifty days in a row was macaroni and cheese. We also had some Logan Bread, which is pretty tasty when fresh from the oven, but gets so hard after a couple of weeks that you have to use an ice ax to cut off a piece. But that has its advantages. It lasts longer because you can't eat it very fast.

"After the McKinley climb, some of the climbers were stranded in camp because the weather turned bad before they could be picked up by plane. The storm continued, and they had to last out a week with no food. They stayed in their tents and kept as still as possible so they wouldn't burn up any unnecessary energy. When the storm cleared, their friends in Talkeetna had food airdropped to them, among it a lot of peanut butter in jars. On landing, the jars broke. The climbers were so hungry that they spent the next few days picking glass out of the peanut butter so they could eat it.

"A really lightweight food is kasha, grain for a Russian hot cereal (it can be cracked buckwheat, barley, millet, or wheat). A very small amount expands to a huge volume. It is available in health food stores. The brown kasha is better than the yellow. Cook it like whole wheat cereal. Eat with lots of butter or with vegetables and spices."

● ● ● ● ● ● ● ● ●

Peter Lev of Salt Lake City, Utah, and Rod Newcomb of the Black Hills of South Dakota are still actively guiding for Exum Mountain Guides—Peter for forty-three years and Rod for forty years. Both are out in the backcountry on skis in the winter enjoying Rocky Mountain powder at its best. Rod is the director of and an instructor for the American Avalanche Institute.

Peter and Rod have climbed extensively in the Tetons and elsewhere. Rod has been on expeditions to Mount Steele in the St. Elias Range and to Mount McKinley's east buttress. Peter has been on expeditions to McKinley, Logan, Dhaulagiri, Nanda Devi, Island Peak near Everest, and the Pamirs in the former Soviet Union.

Wayne Merry

Mishaps and Merryment

"I am all for simple meals. On long trips I like to eat the same thing every day. For breakfast I like a hot drink made from chocolate-flavored malt beverage mix and instant coffee. Most of my dinners are one-pot affairs with an instant pudding for dessert. This is not the case, of course, when I'm leading a paid trek!

"A neglected 'meal' is the so-called midnight snack. There's a terrible time, usually about 4 A.M., when you wake up cold and can't get back to sleep. Your blood sugar is low, metabolism down, and the night is at its coldest. The magic medicine is a good hunk of chocolate. It kicks up your blood sugar, and soon you'll be asleep again, cozy and contented. Just don't tell your dentist.

"One winter in Mount McKinley National Park, three of us went out on a four-day snowshoe trip. In an old patrol cabin with a functional wood stove, I mixed up a huge pan of dried eggs and set the rather liquid batter by the stove, ready for a quick breakfast next day. But in the morning there was something in the batter—one of my oldest felt mukluk insoles that I had hung over the stove to dry. It had been marinating all night. However, no one else had seen this, and as we were a bit short of food I scraped off the excess batter and scrambled the eggs. To explain the flavor, I commented that the eggs were a bit burned.

"Later, I wrote one of the guys and told him all. The following Christmas he sent me a bag of 'super trail food' that he said his wife had developed. I was a little suspicious, but it looked like chocolate-covered bridge mix and smelled good; so next day I took the bag along on a climb I was guiding. I offered my client a piece and took one myself. We both bit into it simultaneously—and spat it out. We had each chewed up a chocolate-dipped moose scat."

● ● ● ● ● ● ● ● ●

Wayne Merry lives with his wife, Cindy, in the remote village of Atlin, British Columbia, where he was previously a wilderness guide and is now a trainer and consultant in search and rescue, wilderness first aid, and survival. He has written several books and many magazine articles and has twice received National Achievement Awards from Canada's National Search and Rescue (SAR) Secretariat. He spent ten years as a rescue ranger with the National Park Service in the United States and created the mountain guide service and cross-country ski school in Yosemite National Park. In 1958, with Warren Harding, he did the first ascent of The Nose on El Capitan, and in 1972 led the first ski crossing of the Brooks Range in Alaska.

Will Gadd

Visions of Pizza and Fudge

"In 2002 I went to Chile, where I was introduced to Eduardo Mondragon, a transplanted Spaniard. Eduardo offered to take me into a remote ice-climbing area for a few days. I eagerly accepted. As we packed gear in the parking lot of a convenience store, he handed me the food bag, about the size of a loaf of squashed white bread, and said, 'I hope you like Chilean food.' Brilliant, I thought — all my Chilean meals so far had been excellent. However, the bag seemed light. Eduardo said, "It's very light, but mucho comido. Bueno." Not convinced, and knowing that I like to eat, especially at 16,000 feet, I ran into the store and bought a dozen packages of candy and a roll of cookies. Had fudge been available, I would have bought it too.

"The eight-hour ski-in was gorgeous, but as we neared our destination, the wind started blowing about forty-five miles an hour and the temperature plummeted. I was hungry. We set up Eduardo's moth-eaten tent and he pulled out a package of dried bits. Soon the tent was filled with great-smelling steam. The only problem was the quantity of food producing the steam: perhaps a cup each of a tasty but rather thin mixture. I thought it was the first course. But, Eduardo said that he usually makes one packet last two nights. I ate some cookies too, thinking that breakfast would be a bigger event. In the morning I lit the stove, and made tea. Eduardo presented a Pop-Tart-size packet of smashed crackers and a small plastic container of caramel sauce. I liked it, but a smear of caramel on a few smashed crackers is NOT breakfast. I polished off the remainder of the cookies. Eduardo remarked that I'd just eaten tomorrow's breakfast. After a stellar first ascent, we had another cup of thin but only appetite-whetting mixture for dinner. I dreamed of pizza and fudge.

"With only a few crumbs remaining in the bag, I led as we skied and then walked out. All the while, visions of Chilean marmots, roasting on a stick, danced in my head. Although a few pounds lighter, I had enjoyed safely completing a great new route. I promised Eduardo that when we climbed together in Canada, I was going to bring elk steak and lots of hot sauce, butter, and fudge. That our friendship grew at all, under such savage culinary conditions, says a lot about Eduardo's good nature."

* * * * * * * * *

Will Gadd of Canmore, Alberta, Canada, is an accomplished ice climber and paraglider. He is an ESPN X Games and Ice World Cup winner. Will has written for *Climbing* and *Rock & Ice*, and authored *Ice & Mixed Climbing: Modern Technique* (The Mountaineers Books).

Jack Powell

Ramen: The King of Outdoor Foods

"Ramen is the greatest food for serious hikers and climbers. It is lightweight, easy to prepare, and versatile. Add vegetables, summer sausage, tuna, cooked chicken, or even an egg, and you have a tasty meal. The first time I was introduced to ramen was on a winter crossing of the Cascade Mountains from Darrington to Lake Chelan. The day before we left, it was 20°F below zero. However when we boarded the train for Seattle from Ellensburg, it was raining on the snow—what is known today as a 'pineapple express.' After disembarking the train, we slogged eighteen miles through wet snow to the trailhead where we slept in a small tent. The next night we camped in a Forest Service half shelter and tried to dry out our down sleeping bags. It was hopeless. The fourth night out we stayed in a tumbledown mining cabin that still had a few dry spots under a collapsed roof. That night we huddled together for warmth. Thank goodness we had wool shirts and pants, because our down coats and parkas were as wet and worthless as our sleeping bags.

"As we crossed into the Railroad Creek drainage, it was like entering a war zone. Avalanches roared and echoed in the fog, as the wet snow and rain poured down on us for a fifth day. We wouldn't have survived if we turned back or stayed put, so we continued until we reached the Lyman Lake cabin. It had a wool blanket, wood stove, and a crosscut saw, and we dreamed of being warm. We cut and split firewood. Unfortunately we could never get the stove to draw, so we huddled together under the blanket. The next day we had to reach the old mining town of Holden or we would miss the once-a-week ferry down Lake Chelan. In Holden, we planned to take shelter in another tumbledown cabin. As we reached Holden, we discovered that there was a church retreat that was open all winter. That night we stayed in a warm guest room. The kitchen was closed by the time we got there, so we fixed more ramen, boiled up with pieces of hard sausage and the last of our eggs. While our down equipment had failed us miserably, the ramen meals were always warming, tasty, and satisfying. To this day, thirty years later, I still like ramen."

• • • • • • • • • •

Jack Powell of Ellensburg, Washington, is a geologist for the state of Washington. Earlier in his career he was a mineral exploration geologist, and later he was a professor of geology. Hiking, climbing, camping, and geology have been a natural fit, and he could never imagine pursuing any other career.

Dianne Roberts

High-Altitude Salmon

"On K2 we found that the food we liked at home was not necessarily what we liked at higher elevations in the mountains. For instance, we found that we had three times more chocolate candy along than we wanted or needed. We had quantities of it left over. We also had thought we would want lots of coffee, but even the most dedicated coffee drinkers found it was not their favorite beverage on the mountain. We preferred other hot beverages such as tea, chocolate, and instant soups.

"The most popular food on the expedition was canned fish. We had been supplied with 180 cans of Alaskan salmon. It became the most successful food item on the trip. We ate it for breakfast, lunch, and dinner. I think we liked it because of the oil as well as its nice moist taste. We never tired of it. Sardines, both plain and kippered, were also popular.

"Besides the trips to K2, I have climbed in Alberta, British Columbia, and Washington. I grew up in Calgary, Alberta. Once when I was a teenager, a girlfriend and I decided to go backpacking for a week in the Banff area. We spent days planning the trip, then packed carefully and drove to the roadhead. As we were about to head off into the mountains with our packs, we found we had forgotten something pretty important—we had come off without any cookpots! Not wanting to give up the trip, we talked it over and thought hard. We finally came up with a successful idea. We removed a hubcap from our VW, packed it with our gear, and found that it doubled admirably for cooking. Innovation and creativity come out of strange situations sometimes and are often successful in the wilderness."

• • • • • • • • •

Dianne Roberts of Port Townsend, Washington, is a backpacker, mountaineer, sailor, and photographer. She was expedition photographer on both the 1975 and 1978 American expeditions to 28,250-foot K2 in the Karakoram in Pakistan. She and her husband, Jim Whittaker, together with their sons, Joss and Leif, recently spent four years cruising in the South Pacific aboard their sailboat. In the spring of 2003, they trekked to the Mount Everest Base Camp with Nawang Gombu, the Sherpa who accompanied Jim to the summit of Mount Everest in 1963. Dianne's photographs and articles have appeared in many periodicals, including *National Geographic*. Some of them can be seen on their website, *www.jimwhittaker.com*.

Peter Croft

Lazy So-and-So

"I am a lazy so-and-so. I do enjoy cooking, however. In high school I took cooking instead of shop, reckoning it was less important to be able to make wood and metal things than, say, a darn good cupcake. Also, there would be lots of girls. I was kicked out only once, for the heinous crime of making purple pancakes. I still maintain, though, that food coloring IS a proper way to liven up a meal.

"Freeze-dried food is for outer space. I like to bring everyday food into the mountains. Cabbage is a sturdy vegetable that doesn't need refrigeration. With sesame oil, rice vinegar, toasted sesame seeds, and wild onions or chives, you can make excellent coleslaw. But slaw by itself does not a meal make because it smacks too much of vegetarianism. Hot dogs are patriotic, yummy, and, with a little forethought, easy little suckers to whip up. Don't buy cheap wieners— only buy quality sausages and precook them at home. Also, buy good-quality rolls, as cheap hot dog buns fall apart too easily. Take along a raw onion to slice and dice, and some pilfered fast-food condiments. Then, at camp, as you heat up those fat sizzling sausages, watch the vegetarians in your group, as they surreptitiously sniff the air. If, at this point, you pull a bottle of wine out of your pack, you will be king."

• • • • • • • • • •

Peter Croft lives in Bishop, California, with his wife, Karine, and dog PeeWee. His climbs include the first one-day ascent of El Capitan and Half Dome, with John Bachar, and the first solos of Astroman and the Rostrum in Yosemite. In addition, he made the first traverses of the Waddington Range (with Greg Foweraker and Don Serl), the Stuart Range in Washington, and the Evolution Peaks in the Sierra. He is the author of *The Good, The Great and The Awesome: The Top 40 High Sierra Rock Climbs* (Maximus Press).

Dian Thomas

Hot Rock

"My favorite hiking and backpacking area is the Wasatch Mountains of northern and central Utah and southeastern Idaho. I originally learned a lot about outdoor cooking on family backpacks. I learned more during the seven years I worked at the Brighton (Utah) Girls' Camp, first as kitchen aide, then as counselor, and finally as camp director. At Brigham Young University my major was home economics. Later, teaching food classes in a junior high school, I was the first to introduce a unit on outdoor cooking. I now travel a good deal. Among other things, I give weeklong demonstrations on the benefits of outdoor cookery to other teachers and anyone else interested.

"I have noticed that the current trend in outdoor cooking is for people to do more of the food preparation themselves; they seem to be moving toward more inexpensive methods of provisioning, such as growing and preserving their own fruits and vegetables, making fruit leathers at home, etc.

"A useful knack in outdoor pursuits is making do with whatever is available. Did you ever cook your breakfast over a fire, in a paper sack, and eat it from same? Did you ever make your own frying pan out of a forked stick covered with foil? Have you ever cooked dinner on a hot rock?

"Here is a good breakfast to cook over the hot coals of a campfire. For each person, you need an orange, an egg, enough muffin batter for 1 muffin (made from a store-bought or homemade mix), and some foil. Cut orange in half crosswise, and scoop fruit out of the 2 halves. Break egg into 1 half of the orange shell. Into the other half pour batter for 1 muffin. Place each orange half on a piece of foil large enough so the edges can be brought to the top and twisted. Place the foil-wrapped orange halves in hot coals for 15 to 20 minutes. While egg and muffin are cooking, eat the meat of the orange."

• • • • • • • • • •

Since the late 1950s, Dian Thomas, dubbed the "first lady of creativity" by Tom Brokaw, has been teaching others how to use ordinary things to create extraordinary outdoor experiences through her *New York Times* bestseller, *Roughing It Easy* (Betterway Books). Since then, Dian has written eleven other best-selling books, including *Recipes for Roughing It Easy* (Dian Thomas Communications), which offers more than 240 mouthwatering recipes for outdoors, and *Backyard Roughing It Easy* (Betterway Books). Dian lives in Salt Lake City, Utah, and spends much of her time working with others on her program, *How to Get a Million Dollars' Worth of Free Publicity!*

Fred Beckey

Mushing Along

"I am embarrassed to say that I am probably the worst cook of anyone you know, or may ever know. However, there is one special breakfast cereal that I discovered a few years ago that others might enjoy. It is made only in Canada and is named for a red river—you can't miss it in a Canadian grocery store. It is widely stocked. The grains included are natural whole cracked wheat, rye, and flax. It is by far the best cooked cereal I have ever encountered.

"Cook it for breakfast, and serve with butter, brown sugar, and dry milk. Add a few raisins. It is truly excellent. On one trip, a friend who dries his own fruit and vegetables brought a good deal of his dried fruit along. So we tossed some dried plums, apricots, apples, peaches, etc. into our mush—that made it even better."

• • • • • • • • • •

Fred Beckey, born in 1923, started his now-legendary climbing career in 1940 as a teenager. In 1942, Fred and his younger brother, Helmy, made the second ascent, partly by a new route, of the often-tried 13,177-foot Mount Waddington in British Columbia's Coast Mountains. He has made hundreds of first ascents of North American peaks, including innumerable new routes on peaks in the Cascades, Tetons, Wind Rivers, Sawtooths, Beartooths, Wasatch Range, and Sierra Nevadas. He has also climbed in Alaska's St. Elias, Fairweather, and Alaska Ranges; the Alps; the Nepalese Himalaya; and in Africa. As of 2004, he continues to climb all over the world. Fred is an authority on both the natural history and the human history of the Cascade Mountains region. His books include the three-volume series ("Beckey's Bibles") *Cascade Alpine Guide* (The Mountaineers Books), *Mount McKinley: An Icy Crown of North America* (The Mountaineers Books), and *Range of Glaciers: The Exploration and Survey of the Northern Cascade Range* (Oregon Historical Society).

Bradford Washburn Jr

Chemical Experiments

"Our expeditions did not use recipes. Cooking was a sort of chemical experiment. When Jim Gale and I were mapping McKinley, we found that oatmeal was the only trail breakfast we could eat day after day without tiring of it. Foods like this that survive the acid test of repeated use, day after day, are always bland of taste and are not necessarily at all what you'd consider 'delicious' at home. Expedition food should be a judicious mix of things that provide reasonably light weight, palatability, easy preparation, and the qualities of filling you up, sticking to the ribs, and giving you driving power. We used the same old oatmeal, beans, instant rice, stewed prunes, hash, chipped beef, and ham—in all sorts of combinations. If you are spending much time at high elevations, bring a pressure cooker; it greatly broadens the possible variety, saves enormous amounts of fuel, and greatly speeds the meal-preparation process. On long trips, some tiny treats and surprises boost the morale, too!

"On one expedition we had unusually good food and were impressed by how good we felt despite the extra weight. I'm convinced that at least half the lack of appetite at high altitude is not at all due to lack of oxygen. It's because you've saved the lightest-weight, easiest-to-carry-and-prepare food to eat up there, and most of this stuff would make you gag if you cooked it beautifully in your own kitchen at sea level! Good food, well prepared, will do more to keep up expedition morale and power than all sorts of psychology and esoteric cuisine!"

• • • • • • • • • •

Bradford Washburn, of Lexingham, Massachusetts, was born in 1910. A mountaineer, explorer, and celebrated photographer, he performed pioneering research in aerial photography, wireless communications, cold-weather search and rescue procedures, and cold-weather survival techniques. Bradford served as director of the Museum of Science in Boston for nearly forty years. His work is showcased in *Bradford Washburn: Mountain Photography* (The Mountaineers Books).

Willi Unsoeld

Lower Saddle Skardu

During the 1970s Willi taught a variety of programs, including outdoor education at The Evergreen State College in Olympia. Earlier he had served with the Peace Corps and A.I.D. in Nepal. Subsequent to that he was the executive director of the Outward Bound movement in the United States. During the 1950s, he spent seven summers as a climbing guide in Grand Teton National Park in Wyoming.

"Lower Saddle Skardu was popular with the Teton guides when I was there. We needed a dish that all clients and guides could contribute to with no preplanning. Ingredients had to be easy to get and to fix. Our solution was to ask each client who signed up for climbing the Grand Teton to bring along one can of soup for dinner at Lower Saddle Camp the first night. When we all reached the Camp, the guide would begin opening the cans—and the clients would ask if we had enough pans. We assured them we had pots for everyone. Then we'd go into a long discussion of how scientific experiments had demonstrated that canned soups were fully miscible in all varieties. When all cans were sitting there opened, we would pour the contents with a flourish into one large pot, stir, heat—and voilà: Lower Saddle Skardu.

"Somebody always brought dry soup, and derision was rampant as this unauthorized material was tossed carelessly into the pot, plus necessary water and any cans of corn, beans, corned beef hash, and raviolis that might have made their way to the saddle. Initial dismay gradually gave way to appreciation of the full creativity involved. The final gourmet product was served up in the rinsed-out cans (which doubled as cups for the breakfast cocoa)."

• • • • • • • • • •

The late Willi Unsoeld lived in Olympia, Washington, with his wife, Jolene. He was killed in an avalanche on Mount Rainier on March 4, 1979. Willi started climbing as a boy in 1938. In subsequent years he made numerous ascents in the Cascades, Yosemite, the Tetons, the Selkirks of Canada, and the Alps. He later turned to Himalayan climbing. His early expeditions included attempts on 21,640-foot Nilkanta in India and on 27,825-foot Makalu in Nepal. In 1960 he climbed 25,660-foot Masherbrum in Pakistan. In May 1963, Willi established a new route on Mount Everest, with Tom Hornbein. They ascended the unclimbed West Ridge and descended via the South Col, making the first traverse of a major Himalayan Peak. Willi was coleader in 1976 of the Indo-American Nanda Devi Expedition that put three men on the 25,645-foot summit via a new route, the Northwest Face and North Ridge. His daughter, Nanda Devi Unsoeld, died of unknown physical causes on that expedition.

Gary Willden

Huckleberry Hahas

"For trail meals, I usually settle for a breakfast of instant oatmeal—cinnamon and brown sugar flavor is my favorite. If that's not enough, I add a breakfast tart or bar. Like many outdoor people, I have become pretty much of a traditionalist at lunchtime. I like the predictable but satisfying cheese-crackers-salami-gorp meal. My 'goodie gorp' recipe calls for mixing about equal quantities of chocolate-covered raisins, roasted salted peanuts, small chocolate candies with variegated color coating, and a few cut-up jelly things such as spiced gumdrops.

"One of my favorite drinks for evenings around a campfire is spiced apple cider. Several days before a trip I prepare the spice mix. In a bowl, I combine 1 cup brown sugar, ½ pound butter or margarine, and ½ teaspoon each of cinnamon, nutmeg, and cloves. I refrigerate this creamy mixture for at least two days. On backpacking trips I put about a teaspoonful of it into a cup of hot cider for each person. I carry the cider in a water bottle. This beverage makes for mellow evenings.

"One summer I had a group of clients on a guided backpack in the Wind River Range in Wyoming. That year there was a bumper crop of huckleberries in the Winds. We thought a breakfast of huckleberry pancakes would start the day out right. It took five of us nearly an hour to pick about one-and-a-half cups of the tiny berries. Well, it is nearly impossible to pick the little rounders without also picking some of the equally tiny leaves. We had such a conglomeration of berries and leaves that we almost gave up on pancakes and had breakfast bars instead. Then I hit on the idea of trying to 'pan' the leaves out, much as one pans for gold. Pouring the berries into a shallow pan, I swished them around while blowing gently at the same time. I may have looked like a fool, but we enjoyed our huckleberry pancakes in the end."

● ● ● ● ● ● ● ● ● ●

Gary Willden of Ogden, Utah, has been a rock climber, mountaineer, caver, cross-country skier, backpacker, and river rat since the late 1960s. He has been a backpacking and climbing instructor and guide throughout the West and ran his own wilderness school for several summers. He has explored caves in Utah and surrounding states and has made numerous descents to the bottom of Neffs Cave, one of the deepest known caves in the United States. Gary, a member of the faculty at Weber State College in Ogden, conducts classes in physical education and recreation. He is also pursuing doctoral studies in outdoor recreation at the University of Utah at Salt Lake City. Gary and his wife, Joan, have five sons.

Arnör Larson

Hate-to-Think Menus

"I liked to take climbers into the wild rugged areas of British Columbia and Alberta, where they could choose and lead first ascents. Sometimes we managed a whole week of first ascents, one each day. I didn't like to tie someone on the end of the rope and just let him follow everywhere. I preferred to have climbers with at least some experience in leading. During the 1970s I guided well over 300 ascents, including fifty firsts and seventy new routes. During those years we made several new routes on peaks more than 11,000 feet high. The most notable of these was in August 1974, when we made a new route via the West Ridge on 11,150-foot Jumbo Mountain, the second highest summit in the Purcell Range. The best first-ascent year during the 1970s was 1973, when I guided firsts of seven peaks over 10,000 feet elevation. Another new route of interest was made with the late Dr. Leif-Norman Patterson of Golden, British Columbia; we put up a new route on the North Face of 9650-foot Mount Killarney in December 1971— it was also the first winter ascent of Killarney.

"I don't like even thinking about food—let alone packing it. My menus were the same every week. I usually just threw in bacon, rolls, bread, jam, honey, peanut butter, macaroni and cheese, potatoes, pudding, hamburger, a canned ham, and whatever else I had at hand. I might have been unusual in that I measured my cheese and summer sausage by the centimeter. I can't stand freeze-dried food and didn't think it sporting to use it. My worst disasters were forgetting the spoons, etc., and once leaving the entire meat supply in the fridge."

• • • • • • • • • •

Arnör Larson of Wilmer, British Columbia, is retired from teaching weeklong rope rescue and mountain rescue courses across North America, which he did for a number of years. Today Arnör is engaged primarily in photography and equipment design. During his climbing and teaching career he developed the prusik minding pulley and Kootenay carriage for use in rescue work. As of November 1992, Arnör's climbing list included nearly 500 ascents, and of those eighty-eight were first ascents and 126 were new routes.

Jim Whittaker

Dried-Out Delights

"I reached the summit of Everest about 1 P.M. on May 1, 1963, with Sherpa Nawang Gombu (a nephew of Tenzing Norgay, who with Sir Edmund Hillary made the first ascent in 1953). Getting the news of our climb to Base Camp was a bit mixed up with food preparation. It was some hours after our ascent before those at Base Camp could be informed. They still had no news from us when, at about 5 P.M. on May 1, a radio check was made with Base by the expedition members who were in Kathmandu. The radio contact wasn't wasted, however: the men at Base were struggling over a cooking problem—how to make mayonnaise. The Kathmandu radio operator's wife told them, 'You take some oil and let it drop on an egg very slowly, so the egg will absorb it. . . . ' It wasn't until 7:30 P.M. the next day that the problems of poor radio communication were overcome, and news that an American and a Sherpa had reached the summit of Everest was finally relayed to Kathmandu by way of Ceylon. There was so much excitement that those in Kathmandu forgot to ask the men at Base Camp how their mayonnaise turned out.

"As far as food and my usual mountain outings go, I don't go to the mountains to eat—I go to climb. So I take lightweight food and dehydrated packaged foods. I just tear open the packages and add hot water. When it's ready, I eat it."

• • • • • • • • • •

Jim Whittaker of Port Townsend, Washington, was the first American to climb Mount Everest, in 1963. He was leader of the 1975 American attempt on 28,250-foot K2, the world's second highest peak, and also leader of the 1978 expedition that put four Americans on K2's summit. Jim started climbing in 1943 and in subsequent years made numerous ascents in Washington, Alaska, and elsewhere. From 1949 to 1952 he worked for the Mount Rainier guide service, during which period he climbed Rainier sixty-four times. For twenty-four years Jim was president and CEO of Recreational Equipment Inc. (REI). In 1990, he led the Mount Everest International Peace Climb, which put twenty climbers from three countries on top of Mount Everest, a feat acknowledged by the Guinness Book of World Records as the most successful climb in Everest's history. In the spring of 2003, Jim and his wife, photographer Dianne Roberts, together with their two sons, trekked to Mount Everest Base Camp with Nawang Gombu, the Sherpa who accompanied Jim to the summit of Mount Everest in 1963. Jim is the author of the best-selling, award-winning memoir, *A Life on the Edge: Memoirs of Everest and Beyond* (The Mountaineers Books). More stories and photographs of him appear on his website, *www.jimwhittaker.com*.

Jim Wickwire

Keep It Simple, But Not Extreme

"I like to keep it simple on mountain trips and always prefer to travel light. A like-minded friend of mine once took that philosophy to the extreme—he picked up fifty-two instant breakfast mixes—all eggnog flavored. We consumed twenty-four of these per person and climbed Rainier via the Mowich Face on the liquid diet with no problem. For variety, we had our instant food hot for breakfast and dinner, and cold for lunch and snacks. I still say, 'keep it simple'—but I've never repeated the liquid diet experience.

"My wife, Mary Lou, prepares an excellent granola mix for my expeditions. She combines the following ingredients: 4 cups quick oatmeal, 2 cups wheat germ, 1 cup coconut, 1 cup walnuts, 1 cup almonds, 1 cup hazel nuts, 1 cup sesame seeds, and ¾ cup brown sugar. It is ready to eat on mountain trips, either dry or with added liquid."

• • • • • • • • • •

James (Jim) Wickwire, an attorney who lives in Seattle, Washington, has been climbing since 1960. Jim has made at least eight new routes, or variations of new routes, on Mount Rainier and has climbed Willis Wall by four different routes, including two winter ascents. In Alaska in 1972 Jim was with a six-man party that climbed Mount McKinley alpine-style via a new variation on the western rib of the South Face. In 1973, with Dusan Jagersky and Greg Markov, he made new routes and a complete double traverse of 13,560-foot Mount Quincy Adams and 15,300-foot Mount Fairweather in southeastern Alaska.

Jim was a member of both the 1975 and the 1978 American expeditions to K2 in the Karakoram. He reached the 28,741-foot summit September 6, 1978, with Louis F. Reichardt; the next day John Roskelley and Rick Ridgeway also completed the ascent. Wickwire remained alone on the summit to take pictures and place microfilmed names of expedition supporters. On the descent he had to bivouac overnight only a few hundred feet from the top. The story of this epic climb is told in Rick's book, *The Last Step: The American Ascent of K2* (The Mountaineers Books). Jim's book, *Addicted to Danger* (Turtleback Books), not only recounts the story of the 1978 K2 expedition but also most of his other significant climbs, including three expeditions to Mount Everest.

Nicholas B. Clinch

Letting Others Do It

"My favorite food is anything that my companions will prepare. I am the world's worst cook. But that's not all bad. It makes for very pleasant expeditions for me. My 1960 trip to Masherbrum was most pleasant from the cooking standpoint. It seems that just before the expedition, Pete Schoening—who had suffered from my endeavors on Hidden Peak in 1958—took Willi Unsoeld to one side and told him, 'No matter how tough it gets, no matter how bad off you think you are, under no circumstances let Nick cook.'

"I didn't know this during the expedition. Every time I reached for a stove, my friends would say, 'That's all right, Nick, just go back to sleep; we'll fix dinner. Don't worry about it.' The reason for this unexpected but pleasant deference from my companions didn't become clear till after the trip was over and I found out what Pete had told them. I have always been grateful to Schoening for many things, but his advice to Willi ranks among the top."

● ● ● ● ● ● ● ● ●

Nicholas B. (Nick) Clinch of Palo Alto, California, is an attorney who started climbing while he was a student at Stanford University. Over the years, Nick has made many ascents in California, the Coast Range, the Peruvian Andes, the Himalaya, and elsewhere. Nick has led successful climbing parties in the Karakoram and in the Antarctic.

Nick was organizer and director of the expedition that in 1958 put two Americans, Peter K. Schoening and Andrew J. Kauffman II, on top of 26,470-foot Hidden Peak (Gasherbrum I) in the Karakoram of Kashmir. This was the first American ascent of an *achtausender*—a peak more than 8000 meters high. Nick was also the director of the 1960 American expedition to Masherbrum in Pakistan. The first ascent of this 25,660-foot peak was made by Willi Unsoeld and George I. Bell on July 6, and by Nick Clinch and Captain Jawed Akhter on July 8. Nick was leader of the 1966–1967 American Antarctic Expedition that put up six first ascents in the Sentinel Range. Of these ascents, Nick climbed the 16,860-foot Vinson Massif, 15,750-foot Shinn, and 15,380-foot Gardner in December and January.

In 1985, Nick and Bob Bates were the coleaders of a Chinese-American expedition that made the first ascent of the remote Ulugh Muztagh, the highest peak in the eastern Kun-Lun range of northern Tibet. He later made four expeditions to the little known Kang-Karpo Range on the border of Yunnan and southeastern Tibet. Despite knowing about Nick's atrocious cooking talents, Pete (Iron-Stomach) Schoening also went on most of these trips.

William E. Siri

Ineptitude and Chang

"I was immensely pleased by your request for my favorite recipe. No one has ever asked me before. And despite many mountaineering ventures here and abroad, my companions always seem reluctant to let me cook, although I believe I have an unusual flair for this occupation. I can only attribute this to the human propensity for perpetrating cruel and groundless rumors. After all, who has not melted a pot while heating water? And everyone knows that cooking packaged foods can only produce a substance that has the color and consistency of mud, and that can be rendered edible only by adding large quantities of chili pepper.

"However, since you asked, I do have a favorite recipe that I would like to pass on to future climbers. I call it Approach March Malaise.

1. *Pour 1½ ounces of a high-quality Scotch whisky into a Sierra Club cup. Add water to taste. If in the Himalaya, substitute 1 pint local chang, filtered through a nylon sock. Use unwashed sock to preserve flavor and aroma of chang.*
2. *Bury 2 medium-sized potatoes in hot coals of campfire. Bake for 45 minutes, or until charred layer is at least ½ inch thick.*
3. *Repeat step 1.*
4. *Salt 1 pound beefsteak, and drop into fire. In Himalaya, substitute goat or water buffalo.*
5. *Repeat step 1.*
6. *Retrieve steak (beef, goat, or water buffalo) and potatoes. Note: Do not use ice ax; burning varnish imparts odd taste to steak.*
7. *Repeat step 1 while potatoes cool below a red glow.*
8. *Crack potatoes with a stone, and add salt. Note: Potato charcoal may be beneficial, possibly necessary, after step 7. Serves one—right."*

• • • • • • • • •

William E. (Will) Siri of El Cerrito, California, was deputy leader for the successful 1963 American Mount Everest Expedition. In 1957 he was field leader for an International Expedition to Antarctica. Will made many first ascents and other climbs in Yosemite, the Sierra Nevada, the Rocky Mountains, the Coast Range of British Columbia, the Alps, the Himalaya, and New Zealand. He also filmed *Man in the Antarctic, Conquest in the Andes,* and *Makalu.*

Will was a longtime director, and president for two years, of the Sierra Club and served on its mountaineering committee. Over the years he was active in various other conservation and environmental organizations.

Ted Millan's Trail Food-Drying Basics

*Y*ou can dry vegetables, fruits, and sauces in a convection oven (with the door ajar) or in a food dehydrator. The key is to have air moving during the drying process, and uniform-size pieces of food. A regular oven with the door ajar will work, but usually not as well.

There are different schools of thought about temperature, drying times, and nutritional value. The temperatures included here are approximate. It is important to slowly dry the food rather than bake it. An accurate thermometer is helpful, as is occasionally checking during dehydration. Most veggies, mushrooms, and water chestnuts dry quickly—overnight or in a day, depending upon the quantity being dried. Meats take a little longer, but don't let them take days to dry, as that isn't healthy. Nothing should take more than 24 hours if the temperature is correct and the pieces are sized properly.

Use open mesh trays. Overlay round stackable trays with pieces of plastic screen (used for screen doors), cut to fit. In a convection oven, use the same screen material, cut to fit the oven racks.

Use solid trays when drying a sauce or a soup. When it is fairly dry, crumble the soup or sauce in uniform-size pieces onto a mesh tray, then complete the drying. This method facilitates even drying and rehydration.

I vacuum pack nearly everything in jars, then store them in an old refrigerator in the basement. This is not necessary, but really increases the *safe* shelf life. I have eaten several many-years-old dried veggies that had been stored in a drawer, in a variety of jars, and were not vacuum packed. They were tasty. I'm more careful with dried meats, yet the smell and appearance tests work with everything.

Gen McManiman's book, *Dry It, You'll Like It* (MacManiman, Inc.) is helpful, and a periodic "Google" search for "how to dehydrate food" regularly turns up suggestions, hints, and recipes. A good website with specific information about dehydrating vegetables, fruit, and meat is *www.i4at.org/surv/dryguide.htm* (by Alice Jane Hendley, Extension Diet and Health specialist, New Mexico State University).

Drying tips that I have discovered along the way:

- **Rice:** Cook long-grain rice until fluffy, then spread evenly in trays. Dry at 120°F. When the rice begins to get dry, break up the larger clumps, spread again evenly, then continue drying. Rice will be crunchy when dry.
- **Broccoli:** Cut into uniform serving sizes. Slice stalks lengthwise. Steam-blanch for 2 minutes, then cool in ice water for 2 minutes. Place on tray and dry at 120°F. The broccoli will be crisp, brittle, and bright green when dry.
- **Mushrooms:** For small mushrooms, clean and slice vertically into ¼-inch-thick pieces. For larger mushrooms, slice about ¼-inch

thick, then slice larger pieces into smaller, uniform pieces. Place on tray and dry at 120°F. They dry quickly and turn into little pieces of fragile "cardboard" when dry.

- **Peas:** Fresh or frozen, place them on a tray in a single layer. Dry at 120°F. They are crunchy and weigh nothing when done. Make sure the larger peas are completely dried (bite into one!) before removing them.

- **Scallions, onions, and water chestnuts:** Cut the scallions or onions into uniform ½- to 1-inch-thick pieces. Leave water chestnuts whole, or slice into ⅛-inch-thick pieces. Spread them evenly on a tray and dry at 120°F.

- **Carrots:** Grate carrots along the long side, or slice into very thin pieces. Slices take longer to dry and longer to rehydrate. If not critical to the recipe, use the larger holes of a grater. Steam-blanch for 1 minute, then cool in ice water for 1 minute. Or, cool 2 minutes if using carrot slices. Spread evenly on a tray. Dry at 120°F. As with rice, when carrots begin to dry, break up the clumps and spread again evenly. Continue drying. When done, the grated carrots will be bright little wisps of orange. The sliced carrots will be light orange, curled, and tough.

- **Potatoes:** Cut potatoes into wedges of uniform ⅛-inch-thick pieces. If cut too thick, they will take a longer time to rehydrate. Steam-blanch for 6 or 7 minutes, then cool in ice water for 5 minutes. Place on a tray and dry at 120°F. Potatoes are brittle when done.

- **Sweet peppers:** Clean and core, removing seeds. Cut into strips about ¼- to ⅜-inch-thick, and about 1 inch long. Spread evenly on a tray and dry at 120°F. When done, the peppers will be tough to brittle.

- **Tomatoes:** Slice the tomatoes about ¼-inch-thick. Spread on a tray and dry at 120°F. Some folks prefer to steam-blanch or dip in boiling water to remove the skin before slicing. The tomatoes dry more quickly without the skins. I prefer to keep the skins on. When dry, they will be very thin and brittle. The juice of the tomato will dry into clear, reddish-yellow wisps, which you can use, too.

- **Chicken:** Use partially-thawed frozen chicken, as it is easier to slice into uniform-size pieces. Remove excess fat. Slice chicken into strips, then cubes, no more than ½-inch-thick. Slightly thinner is better. Marinate in whatever sauce you like, in the refrigerator. (I have a vacuum packer, so I put the chicken and marinade in a quart jar in a vacuum. The chicken really sucks up the marinade.) Remove chicken and drain excess marinade. Spread chicken pieces evenly on a tray. Dry at 110°F to 120°F. When done, the chicken will be dry and lightweight, and stiff but bendable. It will have the consistency of jerky.

- **Ham:** Cut ham into small chunks or cubes, about ⅛- to ¼-inch thick. Spread evenly on a tray and dry at 120°F. Stir the pieces occasionally to expose all sides to air.

- **Eggs:** It has been said that you can do it, and I have tried mightily, but I have not been able to dry fresh eggs that will successfully rehydrate. In addition, food safety is an issue, and I don't like to take chances. When liquid eggs are required, I use the purchased powdered egg mixes. Mix the powder with water in a resealable plastic bag, massaging the liquid in the bag to get rid of all the clumps. You can also sprinkle powdered eggs into the pot of whatever you are cooking and they will rehydrate in the excess liquid.

Trail Food Lore

*I*n case you have wondered about the origin of some of the popular trail foods, here is a bit of lore. If you want more information, on a rainy day when you're at your computer, "Google" the words and you will be amazed at how much you find.

Bannock

According to *Merriam-Webster's Eleventh Edition*, the definition is: "an unleavened flat bread or biscuit made with oatmeal or barley meal . . . " or, "a thin cake baked on a griddle."

The *Oxford English Dictionary's* definition is: "flat, usually unleavened bread first made in Scotland and Northern England dating to 1000 A.D."

On the Internet, *homebakingco.com* includes a section about food history. There is reference to bannock in the history of scones: "The scone derives from the Scottish bannock which was a soft cake of barley meal baked on an iron plate known as a girdle, the forerunner to the hotplate. The bannock was round and cut into four pieces, making it easier to turn over during baking. When cut, the individual triangle of bannock was now a scone. The introduction of bicarbonate of soda, buttermilk (which contains lactic acid), and wheat flours meant a softer more aerated scone evolved. Today we have an array of scone variants; butter, wholemeal, savoury, cheese, fruited, chocolate, drop, honey, treacle, potato to name but a few."

Gorp

"Good old raisins and peanuts."

According to *Merriam-Webster's Eleventh Edition*, the origin is not known; neither is the length of time the word was used in spoken English before it was recorded in written language, in 1968. The definition is: "a snack consisting of high-energy food (as raisins and nuts)."

The definition from the *American Heritage Dictionary's Fourth Edition* is: "a mixture of high-energy foods, such as nuts and dried fruit, eaten as a snack."

Thinking that we'd find more about who coined the word and when, we "Googled" the word "gorp" and found links to many Internet sites, a few chatroom conversations, but no information about its origin. If you can shed light on the origin of gorp, please write to Kerry Smith, care of Mountaineers Books.

Grog

The definition found in *The New Food Lover's Companion*, Second Edition, by Sharon Tyler Herbst (Barron's Educational Series, 1995) is: "a hot drink made with rum, a sweetener such as sugar or honey, and boiling water. Grog is served in a ceramic or glass mug and often garnished with a slice of lemon and a few whole cloves. It has long been considered a curative for colds but is generally consumed simply for its pleasure- and warmth-giving properties."

The drink's origin is described in *Nelson's Blood: The Story of Naval Rum*, by James Pack (Naval Institute Press, 1982): "British Vice-Admiral Edward Vernon (1684–1757) is known as the father of grog. Vernon was a noted seaman, and victorious at Porto Bello. He was also a constant critic of the Admiralty and a supporter of better conditions aboard ships. He advocated better treatment of sailors. His sailors gave him the name of "Old Grog" because of a waterproof boat cloak he wore. The boat cloak was made of grogam, a thick material, which was a combination of silk, mohair, and wool. Grogam was often stiffened with gum.

"By Vernon's time straight rum was commonly issued to sailors aboard ship—and drunkenness and lack of discipline were common problems. On August 21, 1740, Vernon issued an order that rum would thereafter be mixed with water. A quart of water was mixed with a half-pint of rum on deck and in the presence of the lieutenant of the watch. Sailors were given two servings a day; one between 10 and 12 A.M. and the other between 4 and 6 P.M. To make it more palatable it was suggested sugar and lime be added. In 1756 the mixture of water and rum became part of the regulations, and the call to 'up spirits' sounded aboard Royal Navy ships for more than two centuries thereafter.

"If the use of grog was common practice, the mixture was anything but standard. Vernon ordered a quart of water to half a pint of rum (four to one), others ordered three to one, and Admiral Keith later issued grog at five to one. The mixture seamen used for grog was named by compass points. Due north was pure rum and due west water alone. WNW would therefore be one-third rum and two-thirds water, NW half and half, etc. If a seaman had two "norwesters," he'd had two glasses of half rum and half water.

"Although the American Navy ended the rum ration on September 1, 1862, the ration continued in the Royal Navy. Toward the end of the nineteenth century temperance movements began to change the attitude toward drink. The days of grog slowly came to an end. On January 28, 1970, the 'Great Rum Debate' took place in the House of Commons, and July 30, 1970, became 'Black Tot Day,' the last pipe of 'up spirits' in the Royal Navy.

"The history of grog does not end there, however. An American pur- chased the rights to the formula for grog and royalties from the sale of grog are donated to the Royal Navy's Sailor's Fund."

Logan Bread

The late Victor (Vic) Josendal of Seattle, Washington, has been credited with popularizing Logan Bread through his description in a 1953 Mountaineers newsletter. Vic started climbing in 1946 and made countless ascents in the Cascades. He was a member of the 1952 King Peak–Yukon expedition, was with the 1964 Cordillera Blanca Seattle group that climbed 22,205-foot Huascaran, and was on a trip to Mount Fairweather in Glacier Bay National Monument in Alaska.

Victor wrote, in *Gorp, Glop and Glue Stew* (The Mountaineers Books, 1982): "This special concentrated bread for climbers was first used by the 1950 Mount Logan expedition from the University of Alaska. It proved to be wholesome and delicious, and has been a basic food on many expeditions to Alaska, Canada, and the Yukon." He went on, " . . . [I]t sometimes sustained life when other food ran out, and it stirred up both controversy and high praise. If dried out too much it becomes hard as concrete; various methods of rehydration include soaking it in tea, soup, or hot fruit-flavored gelatin. The recipe has survived many years of use, and seems to be here to stay—for better or worse."

The late Keith Hart of Auk Bay, Alaska, was on the first ascents of 17,130-foot King Peak in the St. Elias Range, and of 12,002-foot Mount Drum and 15,030-foot University Peak in the Wrangells. In *Gorp, Glop and Glue Stew* he wrote, "This is the origin of Logan Bread—or as much of it as I know. In 1950, Gordon Herreid was the leader of the University of Alaska party to climb Mount Logan (19,850 feet elevation in the southwest Yukon Territory of Canada). Herreid induced a now-forgotten baker in Fairbanks to make an indestructible high-energy 'bread' for the group. One of the other members of the Logan party, Alston (Al) Paige, was the leader of the 1952 University of Alaska climb of King Peak. It was Al who introduced me to Logan Bread. For a couple of years thereafter I was an advocate of the bread. The stuff was baked to the texture of charcoal briquettes. We would tenderize the chunks with an ice ax, or by dunking in hot liquids. (Before tenderizing, they could be used in place of rocks for driving off bears.) Around 1956 or 1957, I had Logan Bread tested to determine its food value. I was somewhat shocked to find that nutritionally it equaled graham crackers. However, it retains superiority in durability, concentrated volume, and long shelf life."

Pemmican

According to the *Oxford English Dictionary*, pemmican is from the Cree word "pime" for fat. The first Anglo usage: 1801 in Sir A. MacKenzie's *Voyage on the St. Lawrence*—"The provision called pemmican, on which the Chepewyans and other savages in the North of America chiefly subsist in their journeys."

In their study, "Experiments in Pemmican Preparation," in *Saskatchewan Archaeology, The Journal of the Saskatchewan Archaeological Society* Vol. 9. (1988), Henri Liboiron and Bob St-Cyr write, "The word pemmican is derived from the Abnaki word pemikan (pay-me-kan) and the Cree word pimikan (pe-me-kan). In the Cree language, the word was originally used to describe the action of bone marrow grease preparation, but later evolved to mean the product itself." Below are excerpts from their report.

"There is no question that pemmican similar to that of today's existed before the historical period. The art of making pemmican was borrowed from the American Indians. It was the major food staple which enabled Alexander Mackenzie in 1793 to be the first European to cross the North American continent. By this time, it was stored in green bison skin bags called parfleches sealed with melted tallow. As the parfleches dried they shrank causing the meat to be compressed. Thus vacuum sealed it permitted ease of handling on long journeys as well as being convenient for storage. It could also be used for emergency rations if fresh meat was not available. It eventually became the food of many travellers.

"The preparation of pemmican evolved over thousands of years, for the purpose of storing a present surplus of meat against future needs. It provided calories in a portable, lightweight, and highly compact form which made it suitable for travellers. It became the best concentrated, unspoilable, and easily transportable food in North America.

"The Hudson's Bay Company bought tons of pemmican from the Indians and later the Metis had established a certain standard of quality. It paid a premium price for pemmican made solely from the best of lean meats and only bone marrow grease. This was called sweet pemmican, which could be preserved for years. The record shows that some eaten four years later could not be discerned from the fresh kind, either in taste or quality.

"Next to the fur trade, pemmican production was the most important industry on the high plains. It became so important to the fur trade that the Hudson's Bay Company sought to monopolize the pemmican market. This angered the Metis who were the main suppliers. Thus they withheld the supply thereby breaking the attempted monopoly.

"Since dried berries are easily preserved, only fat or bone marrow grease had to be melted and stored away in a sealed container if it was not used right away. To store pemmican, the use of hide containers sealed with hot tallow is mandatory. In a modern context it can be said that packaged pemmican was the forerunner to the canning principle and process in North America."

Peppernuts

The definition of peppernuts, found in *The New Food Lover's Companion*, Second Edition, by Sharon Tyler Herbst (Barron's Educational Series, 1995) is: "traditionally served at Christmastime, *pfeffernüesse* (German for 'peppernuts') are very popular in many European countries. Scandinavians call the cookies *pepperkaker* in Norway, *pepparnotter* in Sweden, and *pebernodder* in Denmark. These tiny ball-shaped cookies are full of spices such as cinnamon, cardamom, ginger, and the ingredient for which they're named—black pepper.

S'Mores

The term "s'mores" derives from "Some Mores," the fireside comfort food. "Some Mores" became a success in 1927 when the recipe first appeared in the Girl Scouts guide to camping, *Tramping and Trailing with the Girl Scouts* (Girl Scouts of the USA, 1927).

They are a sweet sandwich made with graham crackers, marshmallows, and chocolate. The recipe in the 1927 guide: "Toast two marshmallows over the coals to a crisp gooey state and then put them inside a graham cracker and chocolate bar sandwich. The heat of the marshmallow between the halves of chocolate bar will melt the chocolate a bit. Though it tastes like 'some more,' one is really enough."

index

about the authors

Yvonne Prater

Yvonne Prater, a native Washingtonian, has been an outdoorswoman most of her life—fishing and camping as a child, and later climbing, hiking, and snowshoeing in the Cascades, Rockies, White Mountains, and Death Valley with her late husband, Gene Prater. He taught Yvonne the love of mountaineering and photography. For the last forty years, her articles and photographs have appeared in many Washington State newspapers, magazines, and newsletters. Yvonne reported on the American Mount Everest expedition in 1963, and she authored several publications about local history, which have become useful tools for genealogists. Her books include *Gorp, Glop and Glue Stew*, with coauthor Ruth Dyar Mendenhall (The Mountaineers Books), and *Snoqualmie Pass: from Indian Trail to Interstate* (The Mountaineers Books). After raising her children, and as a grandmother, Yvonne obtained her college degree in 1995, forty-four years after she started. Today she lives in Ellensburg, Washington, and writes about rural eastern Washington in a monthly publication, *Ruralite Magazine*.

Ruth Dyar Mendenhall

Ruth Dyar Mendenhall (1912–1989) happily combined mountaineering, rock climbing, skiing, fishing, backpacking, and outdoor cookery for more than three decades, in wild parts of the western United States and Canada, and elsewhere. She had numerous first ascents to her credit. Her experiences resulted in articles in *Summit, Desert, National Parks,* and other outdoor magazines. She was on the board of directors of the American Alpine Club and was the editor of the club's *News* for several years. Ruth's culinary expertise was given wide exposure in two previous books, *Backpack Cookery* and *Backpack Techniques* (both published by La Siesta Press); she also authored, with her husband, John, *Introduction to Rock and Mountain Climbing* and *Beginner's Guide to Rock and Mountain Climbing* (both published by Stackpole Books).

Kerry I. Smith

Kerry I. Smith is a freelance writer and editor who enjoys cooking, traveling, spending time with family and friends, and the great outdoors. She lives on Bainbridge Island, Washington, with her husband, Chris, and their parrot, Gypsy.

THE MOUNTAINEERS, founded in 1906, is a nonprofit outdoor activity and conservation club, whose mission is "to explore, study, preserve, and enjoy the natural beauty of the outdoors. . . . " Based in Seattle, Washington, the club is now the third-largest such organization in the United States, with seven branches throughout Washington State.

The Mountaineers sponsors both classes and year-round outdoor activities in the Pacific Northwest, which include hiking, mountain climbing, ski-touring, snowshoeing, bicycling, camping, kayaking, nature study, sailing, and adventure travel. The club's conservation division supports environmental causes through educational activities, sponsoring legislation, and presenting informational programs.

All club activities are led by skilled, experienced instructors, who are dedicated to promoting safe and responsible enjoyment and preservation of the outdoors.

If you would like to participate in these organized outdoor activities or the club's programs, consider a membership in The Mountaineers. For information and an application, write or call The Mountaineers, Club Headquarters, 300 Third Avenue West, Seattle, WA 98119; 206-284-6310. You can also visit the club's website at *www.mountaineers.org* or contact The Mountaineers via email at *clubmail@mountaineers.org.*

The Mountaineers Books, an active, nonprofit publishing program of the club, produces guidebooks, instructional texts, historical works, natural history guides, and works on environmental conservation. All books produced by The Mountaineers Books fulfill the club's mission.

Send or call for our catalog of more than 500 outdoor titles:

The Mountaineers Books
1001 SW Klickitat Way, Suite 201
Seattle, WA 98134
800-553-4453
mbooks@mountaineersbooks.org
www.mountaineersbooks.org

 The Mountaineers Books is proud to be a corporate sponsor of The Leave No Trace Center for Outdoor Ethics, whose mission is to promote and inspire responsible outdoor recreation through education, research, and partnerships. The Leave No Trace program is focused specifically on human-powered (nonmotorized) recreation.

Leave No Trace strives to educate visitors about the nature of their recreational impacts, as well as offer techniques to prevent and minimize such impacts. Leave No Trace is best understood as an educational and ethical program, not as a set of rules and regulations.

For more information, visit *www.LNT.org,* or call 800-332-4100.

OTHER TITLES YOU MIGHT ENJOY FROM
THE MOUNTAINEERS BOOKS

Backcountry Cooking: From Pack to Plate in 10 Minutes, *Dorcas Miller*
Over 144 recipes and how to plan simple meals.

More Backcountry Cooking: Moveable Feasts from the Experts
Dorcas Miller
Practical, tasty recipes that are quick, easy, and nutritious.

Everyday Wisdom: 1001 Expert Tips for Hikers
Karen Berger
Expert tips and tricks for hikers and backpackers selected from one of the most popular *Backpacker* magazine columns.

Don't Forget the Duct Tape: Tips and Tricks for Repairing Outdoor Gear
Kristin Hostetter
Pack this little guide with you and be an outdoor fixit guru!

Photography Outdoors: A Field Guide for Travel and Adventure Photographers
Mark Gardner & Art Wolfe
Learn to capture outdoor images of whimsy and magnificence.

Digital Photography Outdoors: A Field Guide for Travel & Adventure Photographers
James Martin
Special techniques for outdoor adventure shooting—making the most of digital's advantages.

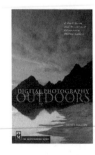

Available at fine bookstores and outdoor stores, by phone at 800-553-4453 or on the web at *www.mountaineersbooks.org*.

THE MOUNTAINEERS BOOKS